OVERVIEW

Overview

Organizations can't thrive without good managers to direct people, planning, and events. And many managers couldn't survive without their right hands – their administrative support professionals, or admin professionals.

Also known as an administrative assistant, administrative secretary, executive assistant, or even office manager, the admin professional handles an astonishing variety of tasks in today's organizations.

For example, they draft business correspondence, manage projects, create and maintain databases, schedule their boss's time, and conduct research. They also order office supplies, work with contractors and vendors, answer and handle telephone calls, create spreadsheets and reports, and plan and coordinate small and large meetings and events. It's no wonder that many managers consider their admin professionals to be their partners.

Admin professionals are often highly capable of operating state-of-the-art hardware and software. They are usually good communicators and are able to adapt to different personalities and work styles. Nowadays, admin professionals work side-by-side with their boss. They also often attend meetings in their boss's place and have authority to speak on behalf of the boss.

In this book, you'll learn about the skills needed to be a successful admin professional, including communication skills, organizing and managing skills, problem-solving skills, and basic office skills.

You'll also learn how to work effectively for your boss by anticipating your boss's needs, making your boss look good, and keeping your boss informed.

Finally, you'll learn some effective methods for communicating your boss's decisions to the people who will carry them out.

Very few offices can function without the support of an administrative professional. This is the person in a company who must be organized, motivated, and equipped to handle a variety of office functions. Without the administrative professional, productivity in many offices would suffer.

Question

Imagine your boss is out of the office. How would you rate your ability to keep things running smoothly?

Options:

1. I know my job inside and out, and do it well
2. I don't feel confident about some areas of my job
3. I need more direction in many areas of my job

Answer:

Option 1: It's great you're so confident in your abilities! Even so, improving your skills will make you a more valuable member of your company. This book discusses common administrative functions such as working with records, making travel arrangements, and planning and recording meetings.

Option 2: When you don't feel confident in your abilities, your performance may suffer. But don't worry – this book covers ways you can improve your skills in administrative tasks like working with records, making travel arrangements, and planning and recording meetings.

Option 3: Many administrative professionals are so busy they don't have time to learn new skills. But having a strong foundation in common administrative tasks can make you more valuable in your company. This book outlines ways you can improve your abilities in working with records, making travel arrangements, and planning and recording meetings.

As an administrative professional, your responsibilities are numerous. They're also vital to your company's operation.

Your job can vary depending on the industry, company, and person you work for.

However, some of the most important tasks every administrative professional performs are keeping accurate records, making business travel arrangements, and planning and recording meetings.

You probably work with business records on a daily basis. This book discusses how you can maintain organization by being able to keep track of the different types of records.

Making travel arrangements is another task you may perform regularly.

This book discusses how to make the proper arrangements for your employer, which can reduce the stress of traveling.

Learning how to perform this task well will also benefit you – you'll be able to perform your job responsibilities more effectively.

The final tasks this book covers are planning and recording meetings. Administrative professionals have a key role in planning and scheduling meetings. It's not enough to simply book a conference room – you need to use your judgment and abilities to help make a meeting a success.

As an administrative professional, you have a vital role in your organization.

Knowing the best ways to perform your tasks can make your role even more valuable and help you achieve greater professional success.

Does this situation sound familiar? Tanya is an administrative support professional. She and her very busy boss just don't get along. She feels micromanaged and wishes her boss trusted her more. She worries about her chances of advancement. Tanya does whatever tasks her boss tells her to, but she daydreams about having more satisfying work. Maybe you know someone like Tanya – or maybe you've even been in her circumstance yourself.

Tanya is right to be concerned, because poor relationships with the boss can lead to missed career advancement opportunities and are major reasons for high staff turnover.

But it doesn't have to be that way. Positive relationships with superiors lead to job success and satisfaction. So how can Tanya – or you – create a good rapport with the boss?

Tanya came to realize that she and her boss are dependent on each other. Without her work in administrative support, her boss can't do his job effectively.

And without her boss's perspective, experience, and support, the admin professional lacks information critical to her work success and career progress.

Tanya made an effort to establish a positive relationship with the boss. She learned how to understand and accommodate his personal management style, and to handle confrontation assertively.

When Tanya became proactive at partnership, she came to appreciate her boss's attention to detail. And he learned to depend on her and understand how versatile she was. Tanya's boss became her biggest supporter, and they were more productive than they'd ever been. Her "bad job" became her dream job.

Think about your own bosses – past and present – and the quality of your relationships with them. Three important dimensions of relationships should be considered: partnership and mutuality, compatibility and the need to accommodate different personalities and styles, and successful conflict resolution.

In this book, you'll learn about building and maintaining a partnership with your boss. Specifically, you'll understand how to establish and maintain the elements of a true partnership, and how you can benefit personally from it.

You'll also explore approaches for dealing effectively with different management styles.

And you'll become familiar with the various techniques for assertively handling the confrontations that may occur over the book of your partnership with your boss.

During the book of his day, Nils, an administrative support professional, spends part of his time quietly at his desk performing basic tasks such as sorting, typing, filing, scheduling, and ordering. At the same time, he's responsible for screening visitors, routing calls to the right person, handling inquiries, and negotiating solutions. These aren't simply tasks, they are interactions. Nils knows that interacting well with others in the office is a vital skill for support professionals.

As an administrative support professional, you no doubt interact with many different types of people in your organization every day.

And you probably interact with regular contacts outside your organization as well. Depending on your job, you may deal with dozens of interactions in a typical workday.

As an administrative professional, you need to work as effectively as possible with the different people around you. While some interactions may be brief and superficial, others can be very important or even deeply personal. Three types of interactions can be particularly challenging:

- Trying to be a supportive rather than a competitive player in your organization requires skill and effort. When you succeed at it, coworkers trust you more and your reputation as a strong team player grows.
- Asking for assistance from a coworker can be awkward if done incorrectly. When you know how to ask for help, you can do so in a way that enhances work relationships instead of straining them.
- Handling criticism is an important skill for someone who interacts with colleagues as often as an administrative support professional. Using the right techniques can make it a positive, collaborative experience.

This book is designed to help you handle interactions more effectively. Whether it's interacting with your boss, a client, or a coworker, you'll learn how to be a more supportive player.

The book also provides guidelines for asking for help, an interaction you'll inevitably encounter in your career as an administrative professional.

You'll also learn how to handle criticism in the workplace. The book gives you guidelines on taking criticism well and challenging unfair criticism appropriately.

When you learn how to handle the various interactions you're likely to encounter, you'll have acquired an important skill set for succeeding in the workplace. These skills will help you meet your goals, as well as your company's and your boss's goals. You'll improve your reputation as a team player and improve your relationships throughout the organization.

When you have a choice between interacting with a seemingly positive person and a seemingly negative person, who do you choose?

Whether you're in a professional or personal situation, you're most likely to want to interact with a pleasant, positive person.

Projecting a positive image is a powerful tool. When others perceive you in a positive way, you'll have more influence. So, you should take action to make sure the impression you make is a positive one.

It's not always easy. And though you may be able to try for a while, you can't fake a positive outlook for long.

As an administrative professional, you're an integral part of your organization. You'll need strong, positive relationships to be effective in your role – and you can't fake those.

In order to maintain a positive image, you need to gain the trust, respect, and admiration of your colleagues.

You can do this through positive and consistent action, behavior, and results.

Several best practices can help you build and maintain a positive image and make a good impression:

- projecting a positive, professional image by building credibility and maintaining authenticity,
- creating a positive work environment by communicating honestly, respecting others, and maintaining a positive attitude, and
- practicing positive office politics.

Implementing the best practices explored in this book will help you to put your best foot forward as an administrative professional.

CHAPTER I - REPRESENTING YOUR BOSS

CHAPTER I - Representing Your Boss

In this chapter, you'll learn about the skills needed to be a successful admin professional, including communication skills, organizing and managing skills, problem-solving skills, and basic office skills.

You'll also learn how to work effectively for your boss by anticipating your boss's needs, making your boss look good, and keeping your boss informed.

Finally, you'll learn some effective methods for communicating your boss's decisions to the people who will carry them out.

SKILLS AND PERSONAL QUALITIES

Skills and personal qualities

Administrative support professional role

Babu is looking for a new job. As part of his morning routine, he scans the "help wanted" advertisements in the newspaper. One day, he spots an interesting advertisement.

The ad reads: "WANTED: Highly motivated individual to work as administrative support professional to a vice president in a fast-growing sales organization. Must have excellent communication skills, organizing and managing skills, basic office management skills, and be a creative problem solver. The candidate must also be dependable, loyal, and adaptable to new and challenging situations. Knowledge of state-of-the-art office management software and hardware is a plus."

Babu has excellent technical skills, but he notes that the position seems to minimize these. Instead, it emphasizes a combination of nontechnical skills and personal qualities, some of which Babu possesses and others that he'll need to develop. Babu decides to take an inventory of his skills and personal traits.

Key skills

As an administrative professional, you're expected to have sharp technical skills. However, it's not necessarily the technical skills that have the most impact on your success.

It's a combination of nontechnical skills and specific personal qualities that serve you best over the long run.

The nontechnical skills needed for success include communication skills, organizing and managing skills, basic office skills, and problem-solving skills.

Good communication skills are essential. As an admin professional, you communicate with people at all levels of the organization.

Specifically, you need to have superior listening and speaking skills, and be able to effectively communicate in writing – through e-mail, memo, and written report.

In addition, you must be adept at both sending and interpreting nonverbal communication.

Organizing and managing skills are also key. Administrative professionals manage a variety of different tasks, groups of people, and schedules – all at the same time. It's important to know how to set goals and organize priorities, as you balance the demands on your time and energies. Your success in managing and organizing tasks often depends on whether you use time effectively. Therefore, time management skills are especially critical.

Of course, you're expected to take care of your boss's administrative needs, so you must possess basic office skills as well.

For instance, you should be able to use state-of-the-art software and computing equipment. And you must have excellent writing, math, and language skills.

Last but not least, you'll need to become adept at problem solving.

The more easily and quickly you can think outside the box to come up with good solutions, the more successful you will be, and the more valuable you will be to your boss. Problem solving often involves a high degree of creativity, as well as knowing the appropriate questions to ask in a variety of situations.

Question

Which skills contribute to your success as an administrative professional?

Options:

1. Speaking and listening skills
2. Organizing and managing skills
3. Basic office skills
4. Problem-solving skills
5. Accounting skills
6. Engineering skills

Answer:

Option 1: This option is correct. Communication skills are essential. You must be able to listen carefully and speak well. You must also be skilled in sending and receiving nonverbal cues.

Option 2: This option is correct. You need organizing and managing skills to be able to keep your boss's schedule and workflow running smoothly. It's important to know how to set goals and organize priorities as you balance the demands on your time and energies.

Option 3: This option is correct. Technical and computer skills are often required, in addition to writing, math, and language skills.

Option 4: This option is correct. Having the ability to think outside the box and creatively solving problems are very important.

Option 5: This option is incorrect. Administrative support professionals aren't usually expected to know accounting procedures.

Option 6: This option is incorrect. A knowledge of engineering principles may be helpful if you worked for an engineering manager.

Personal qualities

In addition to key skills, such as the ability to communicate well and manage several tasks, there are some personal qualities that contribute to your success as an admin professional. These qualities include dependability, loyalty, adaptability, and punctuality.

See each personal quality to learn more.

Dependability

How successful do you think you'd be if you called in sick whenever you had a twinge or an ache? Or if you refused to work overtime on occasion to support your boss's needs?

Dependability means that you're present, ready, and willing to take on challenges. Loyalty

You can show loyalty by focusing on your boss's successes when talking with team members, and by informing the boss of issues that may affect him or her.

Loyalty also entails keeping confidences. You're likely to have access to personal and private information, and you must treat it with discretion.

Adaptability

Another important personal quality is adaptability. You need to be flexible and open to new challenges and situations. Adaptable people are able to learn new things. Don't be afraid to experiment with new techniques, tools, and methods that could help you do your job.

And try to be open to change. Things change, and you don't want to get flustered whenever this happens. You can then retain the new skills that help you become more effective and efficient, while building a comprehensive tool kit for success.

Punctuality

Don't underestimate the importance of simple punctuality. Chronic lateness can be a tip-off to your boss that you aren't truly interested in your work.

It may seem a small matter, but being on time can indicate that you're organized and enthusiastic, among other things. And it's something that your boss will appreciate. It will build the boss's trust in you.

Question

Which personal qualities are key for your success as an administrative support professional?

Options:

1. Punctuality
2. Dependability
3. Loyalty
4. Adaptability
5. Submissiveness
6. Self-awareness

Answer:

Option 1: This option is correct. Being on time will encourage your boss to trust you.

Option 2: This option is correct. Going the extra mile to meet your boss's needs will help the boss – and you – succeed.

Option 3: This option is correct. You show loyalty by consistently supporting your boss and the organization, and by keeping important or sensitive information confidential.

Option 4: This option is correct. Your ability to "go with the flow" and deal with change is very important. Change is inevitable, and you can't afford to get flustered when it occurs.

Option 5: This option is incorrect. Submissiveness can look like weakness and isn't a desirable personal trait.

Option 6: This option is incorrect. Self-awareness is important for many reasons, but it isn't a critical quality for administrative support personnel.

Your success as an admin professional depends on whether you have a specific set of skills and personal qualities. These include communication skills, such as listening, speaking, and writing; and organizing and managing skills, including time management, problem-solving, and basic office skills.

There are also four personal qualities that contribute to success. They are dependability, loyalty, adaptability, and punctuality.

It's important for you to take inventory of your skills and personal qualities so that you can work on areas that represent development opportunities.

MEETING THE NEEDS OF YOUR BOSS

Meeting the needs of your boss

Anticipating your boss's needs

There's no such thing as job security, but there is one sure-fire way to remain important to the organization – become essential to your boss. This means that you become your boss's partner in the pursuit of excellence. You are a trusted member of the boss's team and are empowered with increased responsibility and authority. How do you achieve this status? There are three ways – by anticipating your boss's needs, making the boss look good, and keeping the boss informed.

Two administrative support professionals take different approaches. Xavier waits for his boss to tell him what to do, and then he does it quickly and thoroughly.

In contrast, Alice studies her boss's needs and routines and stays one step ahead. When her boss wants something, Alice is ready and usually has it available.

Question

Which admin professional is better at anticipating the boss's needs?

Options:

1. Xavier
2. Alice

Answer:

Alice is better at anticipating the boss's needs. She's proactive, meaning that she works at figuring out what her boss will need and when he'll need it. This enables Alice to anticipate the boss's needs and be ready. By contrast, Xavier is reactive. He waits until he's told what the boss needs.

By being proactive, Alice shows her boss that she's eager to be part of the team and that she'll go the extra mile. Alice uses three strategies to anticipate her boss's needs: she keeps a thorough and organized planner, maintains records, and holds debriefing sessions.

Alice keeps a thorough and organized planner of Kendra's – her boss's – activities. Each Monday, Alice reviews the week's schedule and makes an action plan of things to do to help Kendra prepare for meetings and events.

Kendra is going out of town at the end of next week. Alice writes a note to remind herself to make airline, hotel, and rental car reservations. She also needs to gather the information Kendra will need to conduct business during her trip.

By doing these things, Alice builds a relationship of trust with her boss. As a result, Kendra empowers Alice to take charge of the office whenever she's out of town. This gives Alice access to people and information she wouldn't otherwise be privy to.

Another strategy Alice uses to anticipate the boss's needs is to maintain thorough records.

Alice can't always tell the future significance of documents and information that come across her desk. So, she organizes and files old lists, notes, contact information, sales brochures, phone numbers, and other miscellaneous information.

Maintaining records helps Alice answer questions her boss might have about past conferences, clients, or situations. By keeping a planner, Alice is able to find information quickly when Kendra needs it, which increases the trust Kendra has in Alice.

The third strategy that Alice uses for anticipating her boss's needs is to hold debriefing sessions. A debriefing session typically takes place after the boss has been to an important meeting or event.

A debriefing session will help Alice carry out any follow-up tasks that may be required, such as sending a brochure to a contact the boss met at the meeting. She can also learn what Kendra's needs will be the next time she attends one of these meetings or events.

Kendra recently attended a trade show in San Francisco. Alice wants to follow up with Kendra, so she requests a debriefing session to gather information. During the session, Alice asks Kendra about the purpose of the show, who attended, and whether any follow-up activities are required. She also inquires about any potential opportunities that may result from the show. With the information she gains, Alice can help Kendra field inquiries, answer questions, and deal with business opportunities that arise from the trade show.

Question

Which strategies help you anticipate the boss's needs?

Options:

1. Organize and file phone numbers, contact information, business cards, and meeting notes

2. Schedule a follow-up meeting after the boss returns from a conference

3. Maintain a detailed schedule of your boss's activities and events

4. Wait until the boss asks you for the monthly schedule and then prepare it

5. Ask the boss to keep thorough and complete records

Answer:

Option 1: This option is correct. Maintaining records ensures that you can find information quickly when your boss needs it.

Option 2: This option is correct. A debriefing session provides information you'll need to help the boss with any follow-up activities from the meeting. The session also gives you information for similar meetings in the future.

Option 3: This option is correct. By keeping a thorough and organized planner, you can make sure your boss is prepared for activities and events.

Option 4: This option is incorrect. Being reactive isn't the way to succeed. You should let your boss know in advance what the month's activities and events will be.

Option 5: This option is incorrect. As the admin professional, you should retain and organize items such as lists, notes, contact information, sales brochures, and phone numbers.

Making your boss look good

In addition to anticipating your boss's needs, you can work effectively for your boss by promoting a positive image of the boss. Many admin professionals believe that to succeed they need to be recognized for their ideas and hard work. They end up competing with the boss for attention.

But it's far more important to make your boss look good. Doing it well will enhance your reputation as a key player in the company.

You can make your boss look good by regularly taking two actions when situations allow it. The first is to give your boss the credit, and the second is to improve your boss's image.

Now, you're probably thinking that it's unfair to give your boss the credit for something you did. It's natural for you to want recognition for yourself, but seeking it could cause conflict. In the long run, your boss is more likely to trust you if you don't try to compete for recognition. And this benefits you in another way – you'll be viewed as a valued and key player in the company.

An example can illustrate the importance of making your boss look good. Jean, an admin professional working for Mark, usually attends management meetings for Mark when he's away on business. Jean is presenting an idea on implementing a new testing procedure that will result in better products.

Although Jean thought of the idea, Mark embraced it and promoted it to upper management. During the meeting, Jean gives Mark full credit for the idea. This makes him look good in front of his peers.

What does Jean gain for this selfless act? She earns Mark's trust, as well as a reputation for being a good team player.

Another way to make your boss look good is to improve your boss's image with the team. Let others know of your boss's successes, or when your boss has been recognized by upper management. Deflect attention away from your own accomplishments onto your boss, and make your fellow workers proud of your boss.

Continuing with Jean, the admin professional, and Mark, her boss, Mark has recently revamped the department's sales incentives plan. He'll be able to give smaller incentives more frequently, in addition to larger incentives, to reward and motivate all employees. Jean decides to promote Mark's efforts with her friends in the lunch room. She says, "Hey, wasn't it great how Mark revamped our sales incentives? He really wanted this, and went right to the VP of Sales to present the idea."

Everyone likes to be appreciated. When Jean talked up Mark's accomplishments with team members, she helped to increase Mark's status and reputation with the team.

Mark also appreciated Jean's work on his behalf. He began to trust her more, and empowered her with additional responsibility and authority.

Question

How can you make your boss look good?

Options:

1. Let others in the company know that your boss has landed a contract with an important client

2. Give your boss the credit for an idea you brought to her but that she nurtured and promoted

3. Make suggestions to help the boss adopt a more professional manner at work

4. Ask the boss to share credit with you for some of the ideas you came up with

Answer:

Option 1: This option is correct. You can make the boss look good by promoting the boss's accomplishments among team members and others in the organization.

Option 2: This option is correct. Letting your boss take the credit will enhance your reputation as a key player in the company.

Option 3: This option is incorrect. You shouldn't offer suggestions about your boss's professional manner. It could cause resentment. Making the boss look good involves promoting the boss's good deeds and work results.

Option 4: This option is incorrect. You should let your boss take the credit for ideas.

Keeping your boss informed

A third way to make yourself essential is to keep your boss informed.

Information is power, and your ability to supply your boss with relevant information can enhance your

boss's ability to make sound decisions.

However, it's very easy to pass on too much information. If you do this, you'll likely inundate your boss and waste his time.

To avoid this, ask your boss what kind of information is wanted. Then apply a rigorous filter to ensure you pass on only the information that your boss needs.

Another important aspect to keeping the boss informed is passing on sensitive information about team members.

In your role as an admin professional, you may hear more about what's happening "on the ground" than your boss, because some news may not filter upward in the organization.

For example, what do you do if you learn about employee misconduct or behavior that will adversely affect productivity? Do you tell the boss or keep quiet?

There are three guidelines you can follow when communicating sensitive information to your boss. First, determine what to pass on. Second, keep negative information to yourself. And third, verify rumors.

See each guideline to learn more.

Determine what to pass on

You should carefully decide which information to pass on and which to keep to yourself. If the information is about illegal or dangerous behavior, you must report it. Likewise, if an employee is violating confidentiality and giving information to customers or the competition, the boss must be informed.

Keep negative information to yourself

You should keep information to yourself if it's been told to you in confidence or if it's just negative information about others.

Verify rumors

You need to verify rumors before passing them on to your boss. Giving your boss inaccurate information could cause your boss to lose trust in you.

To make accurate business decisions, you need to keep your boss well informed.

You play a very important role in the success of your company when you ensure that your boss receives necessary information. This is because your boss will perform better with key information. In turn, the organization benefits, and so do you.

Question

Which are effective ways to communicate information to your boss?

Options:

1. Tell the boss about a team member whose behavior is becoming increasingly erratic and potentially dangerous to others

2. When you hear through the grapevine that a team member is stealing office supplies, find out whether the rumor is true before reporting it to your boss

3. Find out what information your boss needs

4. Report a negative comment you overheard about a company director

5. Make sure to pass on all information about other companies in your industry

Answer:

Option 1: This option is correct. You must immediately report behavior that could endanger others.

Option 2: This option is correct. Verify all rumors so that you don't give your boss inaccurate information.

Option 3: This option is correct. You should avoid inundating your boss with information that isn't needed. Ask what the boss requires and then only provide that information.

Option 4: This option is incorrect. While it's tempting to share such comments, avoid doing so. Negative comments that you overhear aren't relevant to your boss's work.

Option 5: This option is incorrect. Your boss may not need information about companies in your industry. First, find out what your boss needs, and then supply only that information.

Question

In which ways do you benefit when you make yourself essential to your boss by anticipating your boss's needs, making your boss look good, and keeping your boss informed?

Options:

1. You'll be valued and recognized as a key player in your company

2. You'll gain insights into the organization that you otherwise wouldn't be privy to

3. Your boss will trust you more, and you'll be empowered with more responsibility and authority

4. Your boss will promote you to a management position

5. You'll be asked to find out information about other employees

Answer:

Option 1: This option is correct. When you meet your boss's needs, you become essential, and you're also valued as a key player in the organization.

Option 2: This option is correct. When you meet the boss's needs, you earn trust, and your boss may provide you with insights into the organization that you wouldn't otherwise have.

Option 3: This option is correct. Meeting your boss's needs makes you a key player on the boss's team. Your boss will trust you and empower you to take on increased responsibilities.

Option 4: This option is incorrect. Management requires a different skill set, so doing your job as an admin professional doesn't really prepare you for management.

Option 5: This option is incorrect. Spying on other employees shouldn't be part of your job.

A CONFIDENT AND AUTHORITATIVE IMPRESSION

A confident and authoritative impression

Representing your boss

Admin professionals can sometimes be asked to represent their boss, particularly when the boss is away or unavailable. For instance, you may be called on to participate in important meetings, to run projects, or to manage employees. It's important that you develop a management style that projects authority and confidence so that others take you seriously. By doing this, you will get things done effectively and, in turn, make yourself essential to your boss.

And when you represent your boss with confidence and authority, other people will trust that you know what you're doing. But how can you successfully project confidence and authority? Some ways to do so are to be knowledgeable, be assertive, keep your cool, and show respect.

See each way of showing confidence and authority to learn more.

Be knowledgeable

Make sure you know your boss's goals, as well as those of the organization. Ask questions if you are uncertain about any aspect of your boss's plans or views. Do your homework and be certain you know what you're talking about before you speak.

Be assertive

Be direct and to the point. Don't hesitate to make decisions if necessary, as long as they are in line with what your boss would do. Trust your judgment, hold your ground, and don't second guess yourself. People who are confident project positive energy and a clear sense of purpose.

Keep your cool

Expect that you'll have to deal with several tasks or issues at once, and don't get flustered. Keep your temper and think before you speak. Always expect the unexpected, and learn to appear prepared even if you aren't. It's helpful to try to anticipate what the questions or problems might be for a situation you may be addressing. Then you'll be ready for them in advance.

Show respect

Be receptive and polite when you're dealing with others in the workplace, and be sure to listen when they talk to you.

Vicki is an admin professional working for Ron, a director of technology. Ron just left for a week's vacation, leaving Vicki in charge. Before he left, Ron fully briefed Vicki on problems she might face in his absence. And sure enough, a problem with a shipment of computers to be used by the sales force arises. Vicki asks to meet with Roberta, the director of sales, to resolve the problem.

As you follow along, think about whether Vicki represents her boss with confidence and authority.

Roberta: It's too bad this had to happen while Ron is away. I really don't think we'll make much headway without him. *Roberta says, doubtfully.*

Vicki: Ron briefed me before he left, so I am aware of the issues with the computers for the sales force. In addition, I've talked to several people about the situation since. I'd like to move forward. I'm sure we'll find a solution. *Vicki says confidently.*

Roberta: Well, OK then. Your department was supposed to issue new computers to my sales people last month. Then you were supposed to provide training and make sure everyone knew how to use the new equipment. The machines haven't arrived, and I just learned that Inventory Control is going to reclaim the old computers next week. *Roberta says forcefully*

Vicki: Have you talked to Pete in Inventory Control? I can't imagine that he'd take your machines away while you still need them. *Vicki states with concern.*

Roberta: He told me that the old machines are due to be shipped to the new owners at the end of the week. I blame Ron for this. He should have coordinated the process better. *Roberta is angry.*

Vicki: That's ridiculous! Ron was aware of the delay in getting the new computers and ordered that they be shipped using the fastest method, at the supplier's expense. Before he left, the computers were scheduled to arrive over the weekend. Then I got a phone call this morning saying there were further delays. *Vicki's tone is sharp.*

Roberta: I expect you to fix it! My people can't do their jobs without their computers. *Roberta becomes angrier.*

Vicki: I apologize, Roberta. You're absolutely right. I'll find out why the new machines are being delayed, and let you know exactly when they'll arrive. I spoke with Pete in Inventory earlier and he indicated there might be some leeway in sending the old computers. I'll try to arrange for your sales team to keep their computers for a bit longer. If this turns out to be impossible, we'll rent machines to cover the gap until the new equipment arrives. Does this plan sound like it will solve your problem? *Vicki is respectful.*

Roberta: Yes, I think so. Do you have the authority to make these decisions? It's going to be expensive if you have to rent machines. *Roberta is relieved.*

Vicki: I know, but Ron trusts me and has authorized me to take care of things. He would want us to fulfill our obligations to you. *Vicki is reassuring and confident.*

Question
Which of the strategies did Vicki use correctly?

Options:
1. Be knowledgeable
2. Be assertive
3. Keep your cool
4. Show respect

Answer:
Option 1: This option is correct. Vicki was aware of the problem and had done research on it before meeting with Roberta.

Option 2: This option is correct. Vicki showed assertiveness when she asked to meet with Roberta. She also didn't shy away from making what could be an expensive decision on her own.

Option 3: This option is incorrect. Vicki lost her cool when Roberta blamed Ron for the problem. Her lapse resulted in Roberta becoming angrier.

Option 4: This option is correct. Vicki showed respect by listening carefully to Roberta's side of the story. After losing her cool, Vicki was careful to apologize before she explained her ideas for resolving the problem. Finally, Vicki showed respect by stressing the importance of her boss's obligation to the sales team.

When meeting with Roberta, Vicki was knowledgeable and assertive. She also showed respect. However, she should have kept her cool when Roberta laid the blame for the problem on Vicki's boss.

Question
Which are examples of representing the boss with confidence and authority?

Options:
1. While her boss is away, Mary learns about a problem with an ongoing project and assertively calls the project team together to discuss it

2. Jon educates himself in the details of a project so he can assume its leadership when his boss leaves town

3. Elliott remains calm when a project member loses his temper during a status meeting

4. Portia allows a project member to have her say, even though Portia knows she's wrong

5. Alan interrupts a project member to correct some erroneous statements

6. Phil learns about a problem that needs his boss's attention, but he feels it's prudent not to deal with it until the boss returns from vacation until the boss returns from vacation.

Answer:

Option 1: This option is correct. By being assertive about calling the meeting to resolve problems in the boss's absence, Mary shows her confidence and authority.

Option 2: This option is correct. Being knowledgeable is a critical component of projecting confidence and authority.

Option 3: This option is correct. If you lose your temper, you can't project an air of confidence and authority.

Option 4: This option is correct. In allowing a project member to have her say, Portia shows respect.

Option 5: This option is incorrect. By interrupting, Alan is showing a lack of respect for the project member.

Option 6: This option is incorrect. By ignoring the problem, Phil isn't projecting confidence or authority. He should jump in to deal with the problem in his boss's absence.

One of your primary aims as an administrative support professional is to become essential to your boss. You can do this by anticipating your boss's needs, making your boss look good, and keeping your boss informed.

You can successfully anticipate your boss's needs by keeping a thorough and organized planner and good records, as well as by debriefing your boss after important meetings and events.

You'll make your boss look good when you let the boss take credit for your good ideas, and when you improve your boss's image by publicizing the boss's achievements to the team.

Keeping the boss informed involves properly communicating relevant information, as well as sensitive information.

As an admin professional, one of your responsibilities is to represent your boss when the boss is away or not available. You can do this effectively by being knowledgeable and assertive, keeping your cool, and showing respect.

COMMUNICATE A DECISION FOR YOUR BOSS

Communicate a decision for your boss

Explaining the decision

Have you ever been in a position of representing your boss in a meeting? Or explaining one of your boss's decisions to other employees? Administrative professionals are often asked to communicate decisions for their boss. You can do this most effectively in two steps. First, you explain the decision, and second, you handle the feedback from audience members.

When you explain a decision that your boss has made, you should speak with your boss's voice. This means you must be knowledgeable about the decision. You may need to explain the rationale behind it and the problems it will resolve.

And you must also sell the decision and try to convince your audience members of its value. This may be difficult to do, particularly if the decision will have negative consequences for at least some of your audience members.

But you should try to maintain a positive and convincing attitude, be clear and thorough, and let people know exactly how the decision will affect them.

See each guideline to learn more about how you can use it to explain the decision.

Maintain a positive and convincing attitude

As the boss's representative, you must be positive and convincing in your demeanor and speech. And be assertive – don't speak hesitantly or tentatively.

Even if you don't agree with the decision, don't judge it or express an opinion that's at odds with the positive impression you want to give your audience. It's not your opinion that's required here. You need to remember to convey the decision in your boss's voice, not your own.

For example, you need to explain a decision about moving location within the office. It's better to say "The new location will offer more space for our expanding team" rather than "The new location doesn't have as many window seats."

Be clear and thorough

Explain the decision clearly and thoroughly. Not everyone will have the same background or understanding as you do, so use clear and simple language. Whenever possible, give examples of how the decision will work out in practice.

Also, remember to give your audience only the pertinent details about the decision. For example, you wouldn't need to go into detail about how long the decision took, or all the people involved in it.

You should say "Alison has requested that we give her our status reports at the beginning of the day on Friday instead of at close of business." You shouldn't say "Alison's superiors want her to turn in her status reports by COB each Friday, so this means we'll have to turn in our reports to her at the start of the day."

Let people know how the decision will affect them

Be honest, and let people know how the decision will affect them. This can be difficult, especially when the decision will complicate the audience members' work lives or add to their workloads. In these cases, be careful how you word your explanation, but don't pull your punches.

You want the information to come from you, and not from the gossip mill that usually starts grinding once a decision becomes public knowledge.

For instance, one of the boss's decisions results in overtime. Be straightforward in your explanation, as in "Michael has been unable to extend our project target date, so we'll need to work some overtime for the last month of the project."

Question

Now consider Sonia's situation. Sonia is an admin professional for Stuart at a large corporate law firm. She has been asked to take charge while her boss is away, and today she has to explain an important decision to several team members.

Stuart has decided to terminate the firm's relationship with one of its large clients. This decision will have a direct impact on Vern, who has been working closely with that client for over a year. Sonia calls the team together to explain the decision.

Which statements are appropriate for Sonia to use in explaining the decision to the team?

Options:

1. "Stuart has informed me that as of Friday, Geib Electronics will no longer be one of our clients. This decision has been made in the best interests of the firm."

2. "When the company's management changed a few months ago, our relationship began to sour. It's no longer possible for us to represent Geib effectively."

3. "Vern, you've worked well with Geib for over a year. Stuart has handpicked a new assignment for you, so stop by later and we'll talk about it."

4. "I've always thought that Geib's new management team was unprofessional, so this decision doesn't surprise me in the least."

5. "It's unfortunate that Stuart couldn't wait for another few months to make this decision. Losing this client may affect our year-end bonuses."

Answer:

Option 1: This option is correct. Sonia conveys the information in straightforward and simple terms.

Option 2: This option is correct. Sonia's straightforward explanation presents the relevant information to her audience, and she's convincing.

Option 3: This option is correct. Sonia lets Vern know how the decision to terminate Geib as a client will affect him.

Option 4: This option is incorrect. Sonia shouldn't share her personal feelings with the team. She should speak with the boss's voice and not reveal her own thoughts or feelings.

Option 5: This option is incorrect. Sonia shouldn't criticize the decision in any way. Her criticism will detract from her ability to create a positive attitude about the decision.

Handling feedback

After you have explained your boss's decision clearly and thoroughly, your audience members are likely to want to discuss the decision. Your task now, and the second step in communicating a decision, is to handle the feedback from your audience.

You want your audience members to know that you're open to what they have to say. Although the decision is probably unilateral – one in which team members have no voice – you want people to know that the boss cares about their reactions and their feelings.

So how do you handle feedback? Well, there are several ways to approach it. They include asking audience members for their questions and comments, letting people express their reactions to the decision, staying focused on the decision, keeping your cool in the face of opposition, and not getting drawn into a debate.

See each method to learn more.

Asking for questions and comments

After you've explained your boss's decision, ask audience members whether they have any questions or comments. Be sure to answer their questions fully and honestly.

Remember that people may think of questions after they've left the meeting, so let people know how they can contact you later on.

Letting people express their reactions

If the decision is a controversial one, or one that has a big impact on people, you're likely to face some resistance as well as emotion from your audience members.

Let people express their reactions and get their emotions out of the way. Then you can discuss the decision rationally. Try not to dismiss anyone's reaction. Accept whatever reaction they express calmly and show your understanding by acknowledging their concerns.

Staying focused

It's likely that audience members will want to bring in other issues that may be somewhat related to the decision. When this is the case, gently refocus people on the decision itself.

Keeping your cool and showing respect

While people are venting or making negative comments, you must stay cool. Don't let their emotions get the better of you, and don't get distracted by their comments. Always be respectful to your audience members.

Not getting drawn into a debate

The decision is not going to change, even though some people will disagree with it. Debating is a waste of time and detracts from your ability to create a positive and accepting attitude toward the decision.

Sonia has called her team together and explained the decision to drop Geib Electronics as a client. Follow along as she solicits and handles the feedback from three audience members: Vern, Marlo, and Steve.

Sonia: I want to hear your reactions to this decision. Please think about the comments or questions you may have. And speak up if there's anything you don't understand.

Vern: I'm very angry about this! I've been working exclusively with Geib for a year, and now we're dropping the company? Give me a break!

Sonia: Vern, you've done good work with Geib, and this decision isn't a reflection on you. Talk to me after this meeting, and I'll explain your new assignment to you.

Marlo: Well, I don't think this is a good idea either. We should be trying to retain all of our clients. It's not a good time to be dropping anybody!

Can't we discuss this and perhaps come up with a proposal for keeping the company as a client?

Sonia: Well, others may agree with you, Marlo, but this decision supports the overall interests of our company. I don't want to debate with you.

Steve: Some of us have been counting on commissions from working with Geib. Sonia: I had nothing to do with this decision, so don't take your anger out

on me. I don't like the situation any better than you do.

Sonia: We don't have any more time for discussion right now. If you have more questions or comments, please put them in an e-mail, and I'll get back to you.

Sonia began the discussion very well. She asks the team members for their reactions. And she remains calm and respectful in the face of Vern's strong reaction.

She maintains focus on the decision and refuses to enter a debate with Marlo. However, she loses her temper when Steve speaks. Sonia should keep her cool and allow Steve to express himself.

And Sonia doesn't reflect her boss well when she places blame on him and expresses her own negative thoughts on his decision. She should deal with the team members' reactions and questions thoroughly before calling the meeting to a close.

Question

Eli is conducting a meeting in his boss's absence. He has just explained a decision about additional overtime being required over the next business quarter.

Which statements show that Eli is able to handle feedback effectively?

Options:

1. When Sean reacts strongly to the decision, Eli states "Sean, I understand why you're upset, but the boss didn't make this decision lightly. Remember that she'll be working right alongside us."

2. When Kate expresses disagreement with the decision, Eli states "Well, Kate, the decision has already been made, and I'm not prepared to debate it with you."

3. "I want to hear your reactions. Please let me know your concerns. And ask me questions if you don't understand."

4. "I don't like overtime any better than you do, so don't complain to me."

5. "I'm not prepared to discuss the decision right now. If you have questions, please send me an e-mail and I'll get back to you."

Answer:

Option 1: This option is correct. Eli remains calm and respectful in the face of Sean's strong reaction.

Option 2: This option is correct. Eli remains focused on the decision and avoids getting into a debate.

Option 3: This option is correct. It's appropriate to ask for reactions, comments, and questions from audience members.

Option 4: This option is incorrect. Eli should let people express their reactions.

Option 5: This option is incorrect. Fielding people's questions and addressing their concerns is an important part of handling feedback. Eli should schedule the meeting so there's plenty of time for this.

Delivering the decision

Remember, when you explain your boss's decisions to others, you should follow some common-sense guidelines:

- explain the decision clearly and thoroughly,
- be positive and convincing,
- let people know how the decision will affect them,
- keep your cool,
- show respect, and
- don't get drawn into debate.

When you deliver a decision from your boss to people who will carry out the decision, you need to explain the decision and handle any feedback.

Explaining the decision requires that you are knowledgeable about it and that you describe it clearly and thoroughly. You should also let people know how the decision will affect them, and be positive and convincing so that they see the value in the decision.

CHAPTER II - COMMON ADMINISTRATIVE SUPPORT TASKS

CHAPTER II - Common Administrative Support Tasks

This chapter discusses how to make the proper arrangements for your employer, which can reduce the stress of traveling.

Learning how to perform this task well will also benefit you – you'll be able to perform your job responsibilities more effectively.

The final tasks this course covers are planning and recording meetings. Administrative professionals have a key role in planning and scheduling meetings. It's not enough to simply book a conference room – you need to use your judgment and abilities to help make a meeting a success.

CLASSIFICATION SYSTEMS

Classification systems

Types of classification systems

What are business records, exactly? Does a handwritten telephone message constitute a business record?

If you said yes, you're right. Business records contain all the information needed to carry out an organization's daily operations. They include all business transaction documents, from handwritten telephone messages to original contracts. Business records can be virtual or hard copies, but duplicate copies of documents aren't considered official records.

As an administrative professional, you need to make sense of all these business records, while taking care that the records remain organized.

One way to do this is ensuring you have an effective classification system in place. This helps you maintain organization and efficiently file both virtual and hard copy documents.

The three basic types of classification systems are alphabetic, numeric, and alphanumeric.

Question

Suppose you need to file records by company name.

Which type of classification system do you think you'd use?

Options:

1. Alphabetic
2. Numeric
3. Alphanumeric

Answer:

In this case, you'd use an alphabetic classification system, which helps you find information quickly by using the sequence of the alphabet to organize files.

Option 1: This option is correct. An alphabetic classification system is typically used to file information that's asked for by name.

Option 2: This option is incorrect. In a numeric classification system, documents are filed in numeric order according to a number assigned to a folder or imprinted on a record.

Option 3: This option is incorrect. An alphanumeric classification system uses a combination of letters and numbers to arrange files by subject.

Alphabetic classification systems

An alphabetic classification system can help you find information quickly because file headings follow the same sequence as the letters in the alphabet. An alphabetic system can be topical or classified. In a topical system, you arrange files in straight alphabetical order. In a classified system, you file related documents under a general heading. For instance, files pertaining to tax matters might be filed under Financial.

Using an alphabetic system can have advantages, as well as disadvantages. One advantage is that you may not need to use an index, because files are simply placed alphabetically.

A disadvantage is that more misfiling can occur with an alphabetic system than a numeric one, due to different interpretations of order. For example, the prefixes Mac and Mc may be filed in various positions if users aren't using the same rules for alphabetical filing.

You may also find that name changes can cause problems with retrieval. A final disadvantage is that alphabetic filing can be an inefficient method for large systems.

Using an alphabetic system is fairly simple. Each folder is labeled with a name, and then each is ordered alphabetically by the name on it. You can then place papers in each folder in chronological order. The most current date should be in the front of the folder. If you have a lot of correspondence with a particular client, use several folders. In this case, you might separate the material into months or years to keep it organized.

How would you file documents from St. Anne's Church, John Smith, Interswift, and 100 Ways Inc.? How do you follow alphabetic order when you have a mix of personal names, company names, abbreviations, and names with numbers?

See each rule to learn how to alphabetize each of these particular types of files.

Personal names

You alphabetize personal names by surname. If surnames are the same, they're placed in order according to the letters that follow.

For instance, John C. Smith would be followed by Karl Smith, then Bill Smithson.

Company names

Company names are filed alphabetically by name, unless they contain a person's name. In that case, you alphabetize using the surname, followed by the first name and middle initial.

For example, Interswift would come before Evelyn Johnson Consulting because the latter would be filed under Johnson. Sonical Group would come last because it would be filed under S.

Abbreviations

Abbreviations are alphabetized as though the full name is used. For instance, St. Anne's Church would be filed under its full name – Saint Anne's Church.

Names with numbers

When you have a name containing a number, you alphabetize it as though the number is spelled out. So 100 Ways Inc. would be filed under "one hundred." And 19 Phlogistix would be filed next, under "nineteen."

Question

Now, practice your alphabetical filing skills.

How should you sort these company records?

Options:

A. Chuck Parker

B. 2900 Advertisement Agency C. Greg's Flowers

D. Gloria Flores

E. Killam, Trite, and Associates

Answer:

Gloria Flores is ranked the first record. - You'd place the file for Gloria Flores first because you alphabetize personal names by surname – which in this case is Flores. The letter F is the closest to the start of the alphabet in this situation and therefore this becomes the first record.

Greg's Flowers is ranked the second record. - Greg's Flowers would be filed second under G, after Gloria Flores, because company names are filed alphabetically by name.

Killam, Trite, and Associates is ranked the third record. - Killam, Trite, and Associates would be filed under K and therefore comes third, after Greg's Flowers.

Chuck Parker is ranked the fourth record. - Chuck Parker would be fourth, filed under P, because you alphabetize personal names by surname. Therefore, this record would come after Killam, Trite, and Associates.

2900 Advertisement Agency is ranked the fifth record. - The last record would be 2900 Advertisement Agency. When you have a name that contains a number, you alphabetize it as though the number is spelled out – in this case, two thousand nine hundred.

Numeric classification systems

Another type of classification system is numeric. You file documents in numeric order according to a number assigned to a folder or imprinted on a record. Numeric systems are frequently used in banks to file customer accounts. They're also widely used in hospitals to file by patient numbers, and in government offices for records filed by social security number. You'll also find numeric systems used for records with preprinted numbers on them – for instance, invoices, checks, vouchers, and purchase orders.

There are four types of numeric classification systems. Select each to learn more about it.

Consecutive

Consecutive numeric systems are the simplest. You number files consecutively and place them in sequence.

Duplex

Duplex numeric systems use two or more number segments to classify files that are assigned a numeric code. For example, in a middle-digit system, you'd use the middle number sequence to file records.

Decimal

Decimal numeric systems consist of ten divisions, which can each be subdivided into groups of ten. The most well known of these is the Dewey Decimal System, used in most libraries.

Chronological

Chronological numeric systems file records according to date.

Of the four types of numeric classification systems, the consecutive system is the most common. To use it, you place records in consecutive order by number. For instance, a record labeled 45112 would be placed between records 45111 and 45113.

Like the alphabetic system, the numeric system has both advantages and disadvantages.

Advantages include the fact that this method is easier to comprehend than alphabetical filing and may have fewer misfiles. It's also easier to expand files because you can assign new numbers without disturbing existing folders.

The numeric system has a downside though. It's an indirect method, because if someone asks for a file by name, you need to first check the index that cross-references the file number with the file name.

Question

Now, check your skills in filing using numeric systems.

What order should these records be placed in?

Options:

A. Invoice No. 87655
B. Invoice No. 26997
C. Invoice No. 87522

D. Invoice No. 12567

E. Invoice No. 57890

Answer:

Invoice No. 12567 is ranked the first record. - When you're numerically classifying these records, Invoice No. 12567 would come first because the number 12567 is less than 26997, the next number in this list.

Invoice No. 26997 is ranked the second record. - Invoice No. 26997 is the second number in this sequence – it's more than 12567 and less than 57890.

Invoice No. 57890 is ranked the third record. - Invoice No. 57890 is the third number in the sequence. It's more than 26997 and less than 87522.

Invoice No. 87522 is ranked the fourth record. - Invoice No. 87522 is the fourth number in the sequence. It's more than 57890 and less than 87655.

Invoice No. 87655 is ranked the fifth record. - Invoice No. 87655 is the last number in this sequence. It's the largest number, after 87522.

Alphanumeric classification systems

The final type of classification system is alphanumeric, which uses a combination of letters and numbers to arrange files by subject.

To use an alphanumeric system, you assign letters to represent major subjects and numbers to represent individual topics. In this example, the major subject is Finance and Accounting, which is assigned the letter F. The topics are Accounting, Banking, and Capital Stocks. These are assigned the numbers 1 to 3.

Then, if you need a file on capital stocks, you would search in the file index for the major subject Finance and Accounting, or F. By examining the sublist, you would find that files on capital stocks are assigned the number 3. So the file reference for capital stocks is F-3.

Case Study: Question 1 of 2

Scenario

You're an administrative professional, and you're working with an alphanumeric classification system. The system has two major subjects – Human Resources and Finance and Accounting.

Answer the questions in order.

Question

You need to add a new topic called "Tax Matters" under one of the subjects. Which reference would you give the new topic?

The letter H is assigned to Human Resources, which has three subjects: H-1 Benefits, H-2 Compensation, and H-3 Recruitment and Staffing.

The letter F is assigned to Finance and Accounting, which also has three subjects: F-1 Accounting, F-2 Banking, and F-3 Capital Stocks.

Options:
1. F-4
2. H-4
3. F-0
4. H-1

Answer:

Option 1: This option is correct. You'd file a topic called "Tax Matters" under Finance and Accounting. The next file in the sequence would be F-4, so that's the reference you'd give the new topic.

Option 2: This option is incorrect. A topic called "Tax Matters" belongs under the subject Finance and Accounting, not Human Resources.

Option 3: This option is incorrect. A topic called "Tax Matters" does belong under the subject Finance and Accounting. However, the next file in the sequence would be F-4, not F-0.

Option 4: This option is incorrect. A topic called "Tax Matters" belongs under the subject Finance and Accounting. And the reference H-1 is already in use in the Human Resources subject.

Case Study: Question 2 of 2

You have a new record you need to file. The record contains information about the proper procedures for hiring new employees.

Which file should it go into?

The letter H is assigned to Human Resources, which has three subjects: H-1 Benefits, H-2 Compensation, and H-3 Recruitment and Staffing.

The letter F is assigned to Finance and Accounting, which also has three subjects: F-1 Accounting, F-2 Banking, and F-3 Capital Stocks.

Options:
1. H-3
2. H-1
3. F-3
4. F-1

Answer:

Option 1: This option is correct. A new record with procedures for hiring employees should go in the file H-3, which pertains to Recruitment and Staffing.

Option 2: This option is incorrect. File H-1 pertains to Benefits. This record should actually go in file H- 3, which deals with Recruitment and Staffing.

Option 3: This option is incorrect. A record containing information about procedures for hiring employees should go in file H-3, Recruitment and Staffing.

Option 4: This option is incorrect. All files beginning with the letter F pertain to Finance and Accounting. Since this file contains information about staffing, it should go into file H-3, Recruitment and Staffing.

Like the other systems, alphanumeric classification has both advantages and disadvantages. See each of these to learn more about it.

Advantages

A major advantage is that codes eliminate the need for long titles. And file security is increased, because a user must know the meaning of codes before accessing files.

Disadvantages

One disadvantage is that users need to check an index before accessing files. This might cause difficulty for some users, and misfiles can occur.

No matter which classification system your office finds most suitable, you'll be better prepared to effectively manage your company's records if you're familiar with all three types.

Question

Now that you've learned about all three systems, match each classification system to an appropriate statement about it.

Each system may match to more than one statement.

Options:

A. Alphabetic

B. Numeric

C. Alphanumeric

Targets:

1. Is an inefficient method for large systems

2. Involves filing documents according to a number assigned to a folder or imprinted on a record

3. Uses a combination of letters and numbers

4. Is easy to expand files because you can assign new numbers without disturbing existing folders

Answer:

An alphabetic classification system can have the disadvantage of being an inefficient method for large systems because it becomes too cumbersome.

A numeric classification system uses the sequence of numbers to organize files. This type of system is often used in banks, hospitals, and government offices.

An alphanumeric classification system uses a combination of letters and numbers to arrange files by subject. You assign letters to major subjects and numbers to individual topics.

A numeric classification system is easier to expand because you can assign new numbers without disturbing existing folders.

Business records include all business transaction documents, from handwritten telephone messages to original contracts. As an administrative professional, you need to have an effective way of classifying business records. The three basic types of classification systems are alphabetic, numeric, and alphanumeric.

An alphabetic classification system is used to find information quickly by organizing file headings in the same sequence as the letters in the alphabet. A numeric classification system entails filing documents in numeric order according to a number assigned to a folder or imprinted on a record. Finally, an alphanumeric system uses a combination of letters and numbers to arrange files by subject.

HOW TO PLAN A BUSINESS TRIP

How to plan a business trip

Planning a business trip

Have you ever been on a trip and realized you forgot something important? Or maybe you didn't plan the trip completely? Forgetting even one part of a travel plan can significantly impact the success of a business trip.

As an administrative professional, it is up to you to plan business travel well. By making the proper arrangements for your employer, you can reduce the stress of traveling.

You'll also help your employer achieve the goals of the trip, instead of worrying about the little details.

Making business travel arrangements is probably one of your most regular duties. Learning how to do it well will benefit you by helping you perform your job responsibilities more effectively.

Although every business trip is different, you might have listed some of the key steps for planning a successful business trip:

1. gather and organize information about the trip,
2. make the necessary travel arrangements, such as booking flights and hotels,
3. prepare an itinerary for the trip,
4. acquire the travel funds needed for the trip,
5. organize the traveler, and
6. when the trip is over, follow up on the trip with the traveler.

When you prepare properly for your boss's business trip, you'll improve the chances of its success. And if the trip is a success, you'll be a success too. Your boss will appreciate your efforts.

And if you travel frequently – or even if you only take the occasional trip – you know that all travel requires some planning. That's why the first step for planning a trip, gathering and organizing information, is so important for business travelers. This step requires you to determine the specific travel situation – the who, what, when, where, and how of the trip.

So a key part of this stage of the planning is finding out the traveler's preferences.

You may want to create a travel profile, which will give you insight into your boss's preferences.

You can then use this information when you're making the arrangements with travel agents, car rental companies, and hotel staff. Dealing with these people will be easier when you know exactly what you need to book.

Tailoring a business trip to a person's preference will increase the comfort level on the trip, which is another benefit of knowing how to effectively plan business travel. Your boss will appreciate that you pay attention to the little details.

The second step for planning a business trip is making the travel arrangements.

Depending on your corporate travel policy, you may be required to work with a travel agent, or you may be allowed to make the arrangements yourself.

In either case, you'll need to book some form of transportation, as well as book a hotel. See each task to learn more about it.

Book transportation

If you're working with a travel agency, you'll provide the agent with the information necessary to make the reservations. But if you're planning the trip yourself, you must contact airlines, railways, or car rental companies to arrange transportation.

A tip when you're booking air travel – try to get direct flights whenever possible, so the traveler won't have to worry about stopovers and connections.

This increases the odds that appointments and meetings won't need to be rescheduled due to travel delays. And be sure to ask about corporate rates or frequent flyer discounts.

Book hotels

You'll have to make hotel arrangements for the traveler. When you're ready to book the hotel that suits your traveler's preferences, remember to consider the arrival time. If arrival at the hotel may be later than 6 p.m., make guaranteed reservations with a credit card so the room isn't given to someone else. Don't just assume the room will be held.

After you've made all the transportation and accommodation arrangements, you have to complete the third step – preparing the itinerary. The itinerary should include the hotel and travel information, reservation numbers, all business appointments, and any other activities planned for the trip.

You should make several copies of the final itinerary. The traveler might want to have all the business appointments listed separately on an appointment schedule.

Finally, confirm all the plans you've made up to this point. Don't just assume the traveler is aware of the details — check to make sure they're suitable.

Question

Dominic is planning a business trip for his supervisor, Lily, so she can attend a trade show in another state.

Which actions would be effective ways for Dominic to plan this business trip?

Options:

1. Find out from Lily where she's going, what she needs to accomplish while on the trip, and when she needs to be there

2. Contact the travel agency the company normally uses to arrange flights

3. Create a travel itinerary outlining all the trip's details, and then confirm with Lily that everything is suitable

4. Gather and organize information about the trip based on the trip Lily's predecessor took last year to the same trade show

5. Create the itinerary and keep it safely on his desk so he knows when he can reach Lily at the hotel

Answer:

Option 1: This option is correct. The first step in planning a business trip is to gather and organize information about the specific travel situation — the who, what, when, where, and how of the trip.

Option 2: This option is correct. The second step in planning a business trip, making the arrangements, involves working with a travel agency, if you're not making the arrangements yourself.

Option 3: This option is correct. After you've determined your traveler's preferences and made the transportation and hotel arrangements, you should prepare an itinerary of the trip and confirm all the plans you've made up to this point.

Option 4: This option is incorrect. You need to gather and organize information about the trip based on the traveler's preferences, not on trips taken in the past. Although you may be able to use some of this information, you also need to gather new information.

Option 5: This option is incorrect. You'll need to make copies of the itinerary so your traveler has all the information needed for the trip — for example, flight numbers and reservation numbers.

The fourth step in planning a business trip involves acquiring travel funds.

This means ensuring that the traveler has traveler's checks, cash, or credit cards to cover the cost of the
trip.

Many traveling expenses can be billed directly to the company. However, cab rides, meals, and tips may require the traveler to carry cash. Don't assume that everything can be billed – make sure the traveler has sufficient cash on hand.

Now you move to the fifth step, which involves organizing the traveler. This requires you to prepare all the materials needed for business meetings. For instance, the traveler may ask you to research background information on the companies and those individuals scheduled for meetings and appointments. You may also be asked to gather correspondence related to the trip, guidebooks and maps, and information on restaurants and entertainment in the area.

And finally, when the trip is over, you need to follow up with the traveler. The first thing you should do is return files and other materials used on the trip to their appropriate location.

Then you can help the traveler prepare an expense report, write thank you notes and handle other correspondence about the trip, and return unspent funds to the cashier's office.

It's also a good idea to talk about the trip with the traveler. Note any difficulties the traveler encountered on the trip – with airlines or accommodations, for example – to decide what you might need to do differently in the future.

Question

Dominic is completing the final steps of planning a business trip for his supervisor, Lily. He's already gathered and organized the necessary information, made travel arrangements, and prepared the itinerary.

Which actions would be effective ways for Dominic to finish planning the trip?

Options:

1. Ensure that Lily has enough cash to cover taxis to and from the airport, as well as any incidental expenses that might come up

2. Make a list of the important people Lily will be meeting with, as well as their positions in the company

3. When Lily returns, make a note of the fact she was unhappy with her hotel and wants to stay somewhere else next time

4. Assume Lily can bill all expenses on the trip to the company and arrange for her to have a company credit card

5. Tell Lily she can look on the web site of the city she's visiting to find out about restaurants and entertainment in the area

Answer:

Option 1: This option is correct. The fourth step in planning a business trip is acquiring business funds. This means ensuring the traveler has credit cards, cash, or traveler's checks to cover the cost of the trip.

Option 2: This option is correct. The fifth step in planning business travel is organizing the traveler, which requires you to prepare all materials needed for business meetings.

Option 3: This option is correct. The final step in planning a business trip is following up on the trip. It's a good idea to talk about the trip with the traveler to learn about any difficulties experienced and decide what you might need to do differently in the future.

Option 4: This option is incorrect. When you're acquiring business funds for travel, don't assume everything can be billed – make sure the traveler has sufficient cash on hand.

Option 5: This option is incorrect. Part of organizing the traveler is preparing all materials needed for the trip. It's not enough to tell Lily where she can find information – you should have this ready for her. She may not have time to do research once she's at her destination.

Business travel is an important duty at many companies because these trips provide an opportunity to meet contacts and explore new business opportunities.

Your role as an administrative professional is vital – it's up to you to ensure that business trips are planned well so the traveler can focus on business, not travel details.

Question

You've learned about the ways to effectively plan a business trip for your boss.

But how does being able to do this benefit you?

Options:

1. You'll perform your job responsibilities more effectively
2. You'll improve the chances the trip will be successful
3. You'll increase the traveler's comfort
4. You'll have the chance to plan all future business trips
5. You'll be in a better position to receive a raise

Answer:

Option 1: This option is correct. Making business travel arrangements is probably one of your most regular duties as an administrative professional. Learning how to do it well will benefit you by helping you perform one of your main job responsibilities more effectively.

Option 2: This option is correct. By following the six steps for planning business travel, you'll help your employer achieve the goals of the trip, instead of worrying about the little details. This improves the chances the trip will be successful, and in turn, your boss's opinion of you will be more positive.

Option 3: This option is correct. When you take the traveler's preferences into consideration during planning, you'll help increase his or her comfort on the trip. Your boss will appreciate that you pay attention to the little details.

Option 4: This option is incorrect. Although knowing how to effectively plan business travel can help you perform you responsibilities more effectively, there's no guarantee you'll plan all business trips in the future.

Option 5: This option is incorrect. Knowing how to effectively plan business travel will no doubt please your boss, but there's no guarantee you'll receive a raise.

INTERNATIONAL TRAVEL

International travel

You've learned about the six steps for effectively planning business trips, but there are different considerations for international travel. Extra research and planning will be required, and you may wish to consult a travel agent to arrange an international trip.

When you're planning the trip, you'll do the traveler a big favor if you keep in mind that jet lag may be a factor.

It's a good idea to schedule the arrival time a day before the first meeting, to give the traveler a chance to recuperate and adjust to any time change.

And don't forget that business is conducted at a different pace in many other countries. Typically, you don't want to plan more than two meetings per day for the traveler. But this can depend on the country your boss is traveling to.

There are two main types of information you need for international travel.

First, you need information about the traveler, or travel documents. Anyone traveling to another country is advised to carry both personal and employer identification documents, as well as documents explaining the purpose of the trip.

You should also gather local information. A traveler should know about the destination area – for example, local customs and habits.

Business travelers in foreign countries need to carry specific travel documents at all times, and be prepared to show them whenever the request is made.

See each type of travel document to learn more about it.

Passports

Passports are official identification documents and are always needed for international travel. If a traveler doesn't have a valid passport, he or she must apply for one several weeks before traveling.

This is something an administrative professional can facilitate by requesting the required forms well in advance of the trip.

Visas

Visas are permits that allow foreigners to enter other countries for specific amounts of time. They're granted by government officials and are required to enter most countries, especially Eastern European, Asian, and African countries.

As an administrative professional planning your employer's international trip, you'll need to check whether a visa is required and make the arrangements to get one.

And remember, the requirements for visas can change often, so double check before the trip to make sure the visa is still valid.

In addition to passports and visas, travelers may need to acquire vaccination documents proving they're immune to widespread diseases in other countries. Be sure to check which vaccinations are necessary and recommended for the destination. Your government's public health web site will list the most up-to-

date information, or you can consult with a travel health clinic.

Some vaccinations are routine, required, or recommended for certain areas.

See each classification to learn more about vaccinations.

Routine

Vaccinations against diphtheria, tetanus, polio, measles, mumps, and rubella are routine for all travelers. These are necessary for protection from diseases that may still be common in certain parts of the world.

In some cases, there may be indication for extra or booster doses of certain routine immunizations, or a change in the routine immunization schedule as it applies to travelers. This is something you can check on your government's public health web site.

Required

Vaccination against yellow-fever is required to enter many countries in Africa, and some parts of South America.

Recommended

Certain vaccinations are recommended for travel in areas where sanitary conditions are poor. These include typhoid and immune serum globulin; as well as vaccinations against meningococcus, rabies, Japanese encephalitis, and Hepatitis B.

Tameka is preparing an international business trip to Mumbai, India for her supervisor Marco. She discovers that Marco's passport has expired and arranges for Marco to complete the passport renewal process well in advance of the trip.

She also obtains a visa, which indicates that Marco will be in the country for ten days. This is something he'll need to show authorities before he can enter the country.

Finally, Tameka checks into vaccinations for the trip and realizes that Marco will need a vaccination against typhoid, as well as anti-malaria medication. She arranges for Marco to visit his doctor to get the required vaccinations and medicine.

Question

What will you be required to organize when your boss is traveling to an international destination?

Options:

1. Passports
2. Visas
3. Vaccinations
4. Availability of language courses
5. Social security numbers

Answer:

Option 1: This option is correct. Passports are official identification documents and are always needed for international travel.

Option 2: This option is correct. Visas are permits that allow foreigners to enter other countries for specific amounts of time and are required to enter most countries.

Option 3: This option is correct. Travelers may need to acquire vaccination documents proving they're immune to widespread diseases in other countries.

Option 4: This option is incorrect. Although it may be helpful to take a language course, this isn't typically required for international business trips.

Option 5: This option is incorrect. A social security number isn't a required document for international travel.

The second type of information you need for international travel pertains to the destination itself. This includes information about the country's climate, customs, methods of transportation, and currency.

See each aspect of local information to learn more about it.

Climate

Climate fluctuates drastically from one part of the world to another. Travelers need to dress according to the climate – this means you should research the weather conditions of the destination area. Then, your traveler will pack appropriate clothes and won't have to make any additional clothing purchases at the destination.

Customs

You should help the traveler research the customs in the country being visited. The traveler should be aware of the correct protocols, as well as the different languages spoken.

For example, the way you dress in your own country may not be suitable in a particular foreign country. Or the way you greet a person may be different – a bow may be preferred to a handshake, for instance.

Transportation

Transportation in other countries can be quite different. Provide a small bilingual dictionary to help the traveler get around. Gather information about local transportation, and find out the requirements for getting an international driver's license, if renting a car.

Currency

Travelers going to a foreign country may want to obtain money in that country's currency. Money can be purchased from a travel agent, large bank, or currency exchange office.

Question

Which are the most important aspects of your traveler's destination that you need to consider when planning an international trip?

Options:

1. Climate
2. Customs
3. Transportation
4. Foreign embassies
5. Local media
6. Currency

Answer:

Option 1: This option is correct. Climate can be extremely different from one part of the world to another, so you should research the weather conditions of the destination area.

Option 2: This option is correct. You should help the traveler research the customs in the country being visited, such as correct protocols and languages spoken.

Option 3: This option is correct. Traveling in other countries can be quite different, so you should gather information about local transportation methods.

Option 4: This option is incorrect. Foreign embassies can be useful for travelers in emergency situations, but they aren't one of the main considerations with regard to local information.

Option 5: This option is incorrect. The local media in the destination country can be a good source of news and information. However, it's not one of the main considerations with regard to local information.

Option 6: This option is correct. Travelers going to a foreign country may want to obtain money in that country's currency. Money can be purchased from a travel agent, large bank, or currency exchange office.

As an administrative professional, you need to make the proper arrangements for business travel for your employer.

There are six key steps for effectively planning a business trip: gather and organize information, make the travel arrangements, prepare an itinerary, acquire travel funds, organize the traveler, and follow up on the trip.

The six steps are the same for international travel, but you must also plan for the travel documents required, as well as research local information about the destination area.

PLAN AND SCHEDULE MEETINGS

Plan and schedule meetings

Carefully planned and organized business meetings can often be the best way to discuss matters, resolve issues, and accomplish business goals. Whether a meeting is a simple conversation between two people or a videoconference that spans different continents, you need skills in planning and organizing to make the meeting a success.

As an administrative professional, you may be required to plan any of these different types of meetings: staff and project team meetings, conferences and conventions, supplier or client meetings, seminars and workshops, and company meetings.

And it's not enough to simply book a conference room – scheduling a meeting requires judgment on your part.

Whenever you bring together a group of people, you must consider different factors – the participants' schedules, how to contact people, and where to hold the meeting, for instance.

Six steps for planning a meeting

Administrative assistants who are effective at planning business meetings follow these six steps:

1. Gather information
2. Book the meeting
3. Notify participants
4. Prepare materials
5. Check room facilities
6. Follow up

The first step when you're planning a meeting involves gathering information. You need to find out the who, what, when, where, why, and how of the meeting.

If you don't have the answers to these questions, contact the individual who asked you to plan the meeting.

For example, things you might need to know include how long the meeting will last, where it will take place, and who will be participating.

Once you have the necessary information, you can move on to the next step – booking the meeting. This could mean reserving the boardroom at your office or contacting a hotel to reserve a convention room. If the meeting takes place in your office, you can use calendar software to book the meeting. Be sure to block off a bit of extra time in case the meeting runs over the allotted time.

The third step in planning a meeting is notifying the participants – this means informing the people attending the meeting of its purpose. Don't wait too long to issue invitations, since people's schedules fill up fast!

You may use the phone, e-mail, or fax to contact participants. And you might include a distribution list to let participants know who will be attending the meeting.

If opportunity allows, prepare an agenda and distribute it to participants along with the invitation. Then, you will need to confirm the participants' attendance.

Question

You're an administrative assistant at a large law firm. The partners are holding their annual general meeting, and you're responsible for making the arrangements.

Which actions would be effective ways to plan for this meeting?

Options:

1. Find out which of the firm's lawyers will be attending the meeting

2. Book the meeting in the conference room at a nearby hotel

3. Consult with your supervisor to create an agenda for the meeting and include it with the invitations

4. Estimate how long you think the meeting will last and book only that amount of time

5. Assume that all invited participants will be attending the meeting

Answer:

Option 1: This option is correct. The first step in planning a meeting involves gathering information. You need to find out, for example, who will be attending the meeting.

Option 2: This option is correct. The second step in planning a meeting is booking the meeting. Meetings can take place at many locations, including hotel conference rooms and boardrooms in your own office.

Option 3: This option is correct. The third step in planning a meeting is notifying the participants. When you send out invitations to the meeting, it's useful to include an agenda.

Option 4: This option is incorrect. When you're booking a meeting, you should be sure to block off a bit of extra time in case the meeting runs longer.

Option 5: This option is incorrect. The final thing you need to do when you're notifying participants is to confirm their attendance – don't just assume everyone will be able to attend.

You've gathered information, booked the meeting, and notified the participants. Now you have to prepare materials, which is the fourth step in planning a meeting. This involves preparing the necessary files, reports, or spreadsheets, and making enough copies. You may want to prepare a list of tasks that should be done beforehand. For instance, you might need to prepare annual financial reports or arrange for catering.

You'll also need to get the equipment and accessories needed for the meeting. For example, you should check that the reserved meeting room is equipped with the right technology. If people will be dialing in from another location, make sure the conference phone is working.

Or, if the meeting facilitator will be using a laptop, ensure that the right projector is available.

It's the day of the meeting, and it's now time to perform the fifth step, checking the room facilities.

You should go into the room 30 to 60 minutes before the meeting starts to check for proper ventilation, tidiness, necessary equipment, and refreshments. And if you've made reservations at a hotel or restaurant, you should also call a day or two before the meeting to confirm the reservation.

During your check, you may uncover some problems – for example, an Ethernet cable could be missing. If you check the room early enough, you'll have time to find the right cable and get the equipment working before the participants arrive.

Once the meeting is over, you can perform the final step, which is following up after the meeting. This involves preparing the minutes, paying bills for the meeting rooms or rental equipment, evaluating the meeting, and processing correspondence. Make sure you don't wait too long to send the minutes to the participants – details may be forgotten if you do wait too long.

Joel works as an administrative support professional for a major clothing manufacturer. The shareholders' annual meeting is taking place soon, and Joel is responsible for making the arrangements.

See each step to find out how Joel completes this administrative task.

Gather information

Joel learns that the meeting will take place on January 20 from 9:00 a.m. to 12:00 p.m. It's being held at the Park Hotel to accommodate the number of people expected to attend.

Book the meeting

Joel contacts the Park Hotel and books the ballroom on January 20 from 9:00 a.m. to 1:00 p.m. He allows for more time than what was originally expected in case the meeting runs over. Finally, Joel agrees on a price for the room.

Notify participants

Joel sends invitations to all the company's shareholders, inviting them to the meeting. He requests that they confirm their attendance so he can arrange catering.

Prepare materials

Joel prepares the annual report and contacts a printing company to make 300 copies. He also arranges to use the hotel's audio-visual equipment for the meeting. Finally, Joel arranges catering.

Check room facilities

An hour before the meeting begins, Joel double-checks the arrangements of the chairs in the ballroom and ensures the equipment works well. He also places a copy of the annual report on each chair and checks the refreshments.

Follow up

Joel pays the hotel bill and thanks the hotel staff members for their help – the meeting ran smoothly. The next day, he prepares the minutes and submits them to the company's president.

Question

You're an administrative assistant at a large law firm, and you're finalizing the plans for the partners' annual general meeting.

Which actions would be effective ways to finish the planning for this meeting?

Options:

1. Make copies of all the documents to be used during the meeting for all participants

2. Go into the meeting room beforehand and pick up coffee cups left over from the previous meeting

3. Return the projector that was rented for the meeting and settle the bill

4. Wait until 30 minutes before the start of the meeting to ensure the room is equipped with the proper technology

5. Send the meeting minutes to all participants a month after the meeting

Answer:

Option 1: This option is correct. The fourth step in planning a meeting is to prepare materials. This involves preparing files, reports, and spreadsheets, and making enough copies.

Option 2: This option is correct. During the fifth step of planning a meeting, you check the room for proper ventilation, tidiness, necessary equipment, and refreshments.

Option 3: This option is correct. The final step in planning a meeting is to follow up, which involves preparing the minutes, paying bills for the meeting rooms or rental equipment, evaluating the meeting, and processing correspondence.

Option 4: This option is incorrect. When you're preparing materials for a meeting, you should ensure that the room is equipped with the right technology – don't wait until the final check of the room.

Option 5: This option is incorrect. An important part of following up after the meeting is sending out the minutes promptly. If you wait too long, you may forget details.

Sometimes you'll need to plan virtual meetings that include people from different locations, and there are a couple of extra considerations for planning this type of meeting.

First, you should use a scheduling invite tool that automatically converts time zones for the participants. This prevents human error, which is common when trying to remember multiple time zones.

And second, be sure that all participants can access – and understand – any tools you'll be using. For instance, if you're conducting a presentation online, ensure that everyone can access it before you begin the meeting.

As an administrative professional, you play a significant role in helping your company achieve its business goals.

Having the ability to carefully plan and schedule meetings and conventions is a great way you can help your company reach these goals.

Question

Suppose you're an administrative professional who is planning a company meeting.

Sequence examples of effective actions you might take to plan and schedule the meeting.

Options:

A. Find out when the meeting takes place and who will be attending

B. Book the conference room in your office building for 10:30 a.m. next Friday

C. Prepare an agenda and distribute it with invitations to the meeting

D. Arrange to have an overhead projector ready for next Friday at 10:30 a.m.

E. Ensure the meeting room is tidy and the projector works

F. Ensure all equipment used is returned to its proper place

Answer:

Find out when the meeting takes place and who will be attending is ranked the first step in the process. The first step in planning a meeting is to gather information. You need to find out the who, what, when, where, why, and how of the meeting.

Book the conference room in your office building for 10:30 a.m. next Friday is ranked the second step in the process. The second step in planning a meeting is to book the meeting. This could mean reserving the boardroom at your office or contacting a hotel to reserve a convention room.

Prepare an agenda and distribute it with invitations to the meeting is ranked the third step in the process. The third step in planning a meeting is to notify participants. This means informing people of the meeting and its purpose.

Arrange to have an overhead projector ready for next Friday at 10:30 a.m. is ranked the fourth step in the process. The fourth step in planning a meeting is to prepare materials. This involves preparing any files, reports, or spreadsheets that will be used at the meeting, as well as getting the necessary equipment and accessories for the meeting.

Ensure the meeting room is tidy and the projector works is ranked the fifth step in the process. The fifth step in planning a meeting is to check the room facilities. You should go into the room 30 to 60 minutes before the meeting starts to check for proper ventilation, tidiness, necessary equipment, and refreshments.

Ensure all equipment used is returned to its proper place is ranked the sixth step in the process. The sixth and final step in planning a meeting is to follow up on the meeting. This involves preparing the minutes, paying bills for the meeting rooms or rental equipment, evaluating the meeting, and processing correspondence.

RECORDING MEETINGS

Recording meetings

Even after you've planned and scheduled a meeting, you still have an active role to play. Another valuable skill administrative professionals should have is the ability to effectively record a meeting's minutes.

When you're responsible for recording the minutes of a meeting, you may want to follow some general steps to help you perform the task effectively:

- before the meeting, make sure you prepare yourself,
- during the meeting, try to sit next to the chairperson,
- as the meeting progresses, be sure to keep accurate notes, and
- when the meeting is over, prepare your minutes.

Before a meeting begins, you should prepare yourself by checking what the meeting will cover. You can study the agenda or learn the meeting terminology, for example. Other ways you might prepare yourself are by examining the previous meeting's minutes and going over the contents of the meeting folder, which contains any information or documents needed for the meeting. You'll become more familiar with the participants' names and the items to be discussed, making it easier to take notes.

Debbie is an administrative support professional at an electronics retailer. She's responsible for recording the minutes at the weekly sales meeting.

Debbie first goes over the agenda for the meeting and notices that the vice president will be talking about profit-sharing options for employees.

Debbie studies everything in the meeting folder and familiarizes herself with the new contract that will be discussed. She finds she can take notes faster when she understands what's being talked about.

Why sit next to the chairperson?

Sitting next to the chairperson can make it easier to record meetings since you can better hear what's said. You can even prearrange a signal with the chairperson that indicates you missed something and need it repeated.

Recording a meeting's minutes can be less complicated if you sit next to the chairperson. This makes it easier to hear every word that's spoken. You can have a prearranged signal that prompts the chairperson to ask for a repetition if you miss something that was said. Even with repetition, you might miss a speaker's name – if this happens, make a note to find out the person's identity after the meeting.

The meeting is about to begin at the electronics retailer. Debbie speaks with the chairperson, Jerry, to let him know that if she raises her pen, he should ask the speaker to repeat himself.

Debbie sits beside Jerry during the meeting so she can hear everything he says and take accurate notes.

Another technique for recording meetings is to keep accurate notes. Record the names of individuals who are present as well as those who are absent. Also, note who arrives late or leaves the room during the meeting. Let the chairperson know when a quorum is present. A quorum is the least number of meeting participants required to conduct business legally or officially. Your company may want this information recorded for its voting records.

Your notes should cover important facts discussed during the meeting. You don't have to record everything that's said.

However, important statements, resolutions, motions, amendments, decisions, and conclusions should be recorded word for word.

During the meeting at the electronics retailer, Debbie notes that there are only nine people in attendance, and the company requires ten for a quorum to be present.

Since she's an experienced recorder, Debbie knows when to record statements verbatim and when to summarize the important points.

For instance, she doesn't note that some of the participants discussed a business trip taking place next month. She does, however, record the agreement reached about the new contract.

Question

As an administrative professional, you may record meetings in many different ways.

Do you think it's appropriate to use a tape recorder to help you take notes?

Options:

1. Yes
2. No

Answer:

A tape recorder can be a great instrument to help you record a meeting's minutes. You can also use it to record important statements, resolutions, motions, amendments, decisions, and conclusions word for word. But be sure to ask the participants' permission before making an audio recording of any meeting.

After a meeting, you'll be required to prepare your minutes. This means reviewing and condensing your notes while they're still fresh in your mind. This document may be a brief summary for all the meeting's participants, or an official record of the proceedings. Remember to write this report in a way that points out the group's actions, rather than specific statements made by individuals.

See each of the four key sections to find out what should be included in your minutes.

Attendance
In this section, you should note who attended the meeting.

Agenda
This section should indicate all the agenda items that were covered.

Discussion
In this section, you should include all the matters that were discussed.

Adjournment
This section should indicate what time the meeting adjourned.

It's normal to feel a bit anxious when you're first asked to record a meeting's minutes. But if you prepare yourself, sit next to the chairperson, keep accurate notes, and prepare your minutes, you'll complete this task with ease.

Question
Which are steps that can help administrative professionals record meetings effectively?

Options:
1. Prepare by checking what the meeting will cover
2. Sit next to the chairperson
3. Keep accurate notes
4. Prepare the minutes promptly
5. Ask the speaker to repeat himself as often as needed
6. Record everything that's discussed

Answer:
Option 1: This option is correct. Before a meeting begins, you should prepare yourself by studying the agenda, learning the meeting terminology, examining the previous meeting's minutes, and going over the contents of the meeting folder.

Option 2: This option is correct. Recording a meeting's minutes can be less complicated if you sit next to the chairperson. This makes it easier to hear every word that's spoken.

Option 3: This option is correct. Keeping accurate notes makes it easier to prepare your minutes later on. Things you should record are the names of individuals who are present and absent, who arrives late or leaves the room during the meeting, and whether a quorum is present.

Option 4: This option is correct. After a meeting, you'll be required to prepare your minutes. This means reviewing and condensing your notes while they're still fresh in your mind.

Option 5: This option is incorrect. Instead of asking the speaker to repeat what was said whenever you miss something, you should arrange a signal with the chairperson that indicates you need something repeated.

Option 6: This option is incorrect. You don't have to record everything that's said during a meeting. However, you should record important statements, resolutions, motions, amendments, decisions, and conclusions word for word.

Carefully planned and organized business meetings can often be the best way to discuss matters, resolve issues, and accomplish business goals.

As an administrative professional, you have a key role in planning and scheduling meetings. You can follow six steps to effectively plan business meetings: gather information, book the meeting, notify participants, prepare materials, check room facilities, and follow up.

In addition to planning and scheduling meetings, you need to be able to record a meeting's minutes. Steps you can follow to do this effectively are preparing yourself, sitting next to the chairperson, keeping accurate notes, and preparing your minutes.

CHAPTER III - MAXIMIZING YOUR RELATIONSHIP WITH YOUR BOSS

CHAPTER III - Maximizing Your Relationship with Your Boss

In this chapter, you'll learn about building and maintaining a partnership with your boss. Specifically, you'll understand how to establish and maintain the elements of a true partnership, and how you can benefit personally from it.

You'll also explore approaches for dealing effectively with different management styles. And you'll become familiar with the various techniques for assertively handling the confrontations that may occur over the course of your partnership with your boss.

A POSITIVE PARTNERSHIP WITH YOUR BOSS

A positive partnership with your boss

Benefits of a partnership with your boss

Just as every administrative support professional dreams of having the perfect boss, every businessperson also dreams of having the perfect administrative support professional. Well, it's possible to turn those dreams into reality. You and your boss can become so well adjusted to each other that you'll work as a team, each trusting the other to carry part of the load in harmony.

The basis for a good relationship is partnership. A partnership implies a close and mutually supportive professional connection – one in which you and your boss understand and help each other.

A successful partnership enables you to feel positive about your job and your boss. A true partnership is a working relationship in which a boss empowers the administrative professional with mutually agreed upon limits of authority and leadership.

Bosses want their admin professionals to be motivated and satisfied in their jobs. After all, if you're happy in your work, your boss may benefit. He may have more time for important tasks, increased status in the eyes of other managers, and increased productivity.

However, there's rarely much time devoted to professional development of administrative support staff. You need to show your boss that a partnership involves mutual benefits.

Your boss currently performs duties and responsibilities that you could be empowered to do. Pointing these out may help your manager understand how it's beneficial for both of you.

You're the one who can make changes to your relationship with your boss, so in a sense, you're in charge. You have a vested interest in the quality of the relationship and how it helps you achieve your goals. Bosses have information that you need to succeed. At the same time, they can't do their job or accomplish their goals without your help.

Question

One of the benefits of changing your relationship with your boss to a true partnership is that it brings more of a challenge to your job.

How much are you motivated by challenge?

Options:

1. I thrive on challenge
2. I can rise to a challenge
3. I prefer to keep things the same

Answer:

Option 1: If you thrive on challenge, a good partnership with your boss will benefit you. A true partnership enhances your challenges in a positive way. Challenge stimulates feelings of job satisfaction and motivation.

Option 2: A good partnership with your boss enhances your challenges in a positive way. If you can rise to a challenge, you'll increase your motivation and job satisfaction.

Option 3: Even if challenge doesn't come naturally to you, you can discover that a true partnership with your boss enhances your challenges in a positive way. Then with each challenge you meet, you'll notice your job satisfaction and motivation rise.

How partnering makes work more meaningful:

A partnership connects you with your boss's important and influential work, and motivates you by making you feel that your work matters. Your job will be more meaningful and satisfying.

Question

Now consider more tangible benefits.

Do you think having a true partnership with a boss can lead to concrete rewards for an administrative support professional?

Options:

1. Yes
2. No

Answer:

Actually, your chances for tangible rewards and advancement will increase when you have a good partnership with your boss.

These benefits became a reality for Meg, an administrative support professional for an environmental lawyer. Meg's job initially consisted of answering phones, photocopying, and filing documents. As she became more efficient, Meg thought of ways to do things better and expand her responsibilities. She initiated a partnership between herself and the lawyer she works for.

Now Meg is comfortable with the research and case preparation duties she took on, and she enjoys the challenge and feeling of satisfaction. Meg is motivated to seek even more responsibility.

As Meg gets more involved in her boss's cases, she understands how he helps his clients. She becomes more motivated as she indirectly helps to shape new legislation to tighten environmental controls in her state.

Meg reaps the benefits of her hard work during her next performance review. Her boss recognizes that she meets and often exceeds expectations. He gives her a cash bonus and an increase in salary.

Question

How can you benefit from a good working partnership with your boss?

Options:

1. You'll be more motivated because you'll feel that the work you do matters

2. Your job will be more challenging and satisfying

3. Your chances for reward and advancement will increase

4. You'll be able to closely monitor the activities of your boss and others in the organization

5. Your increased empowerment means your boss will have less authority and control over you

Answer:

Option 1: This is a correct option. One of the benefits of establishing a partnership with your boss is that it increases motivation. When you feel that the work you do matters, you naturally want to do more of it.

Option 2: This is a correct option. As you take on more and varied duties and responsibilities, your job becomes more challenging and satisfying. You become passionate about what you do and about producing the kind of work that really matters.

Option 3: This is a correct option. You'll reap the benefits of your hard work during performance reviews. Your boss will recognize that you meet and often exceed expectations, increasing your chances for reward and advancement.

Option 4: This is an incorrect option. It's not your job to closely monitor the activities of your boss and others in the organization. However, you'll have greater job satisfaction from knowing what you're doing matters.

Option 5: This is an incorrect option. Your boss won't necessarily have less authority and control over you. Your work will become more meaningful and rewarding, however.

Building a partnership with your boss

Now you know the benefits of having a true partnership with your boss. But how can you build or maintain such a relationship? The bedrock foundation of a good partnership is understanding and accommodation.

To partner with your boss, you need to understand yourself, your boss, and the context of your relationship. After all, your success at work is not all about you.

You need to be able to appreciate your boss's goals and pressures as well as any areas of strengths and challenges. Only with this understanding can you properly prioritize your boss's needs.

Of course, partnerships go both ways and involve give and take, but this topic will focus on what you can do as an admin professional.

Partnering with your boss involves understanding any likes and dislikes and accommodating personality and management styles.

When you know your own and your boss's preferences, objectives, and preferred style of working, you can modify your work habits accordingly. You'll be able to find a way to work together that fits both of you and has unambiguous mutual expectations.

For instance, if you don't know that your boss prefers to get information through memos instead of phone calls, or whether she thrives under pressure or dislikes it, you'll inevitably create unnecessary conflict and misunderstanding.

Matching the boss's priorities:

You may have come across many different examples of this concept. For instance, when you understand what makes your boss valuable to her boss – or what the hot issue is at your company – you can focus on that to help her shine. Or when you know your boss's pet peeve, you know what to avoid.

The bottom line is that when you know what your boss's biggest issues are, you have a chance to help solve them by providing the right information at the right time.

Understanding and accommodation underlie each of the five necessary practical elements of an effective partnership. These are compatible work styles, mutual expectations, effective information flow, dependability, and the good use of time and other resources.

Each element of an effective partnership can provide benefits to both you and your boss.

Rico is an administrative support professional in a software company. His new boss, the department manager, comes from a company with a more formal work style. Rico is used to a looser, more casual approach.

Compatible work styles

A good working partnership accommodates differences in work styles and makes them compatible. For instance, people process information differently.

You might need to adjust your information-delivery style to your boss's preferred way to receive information. Some bosses like to get information in a report so that they can study it, and others like to have information presented to them so they can ask questions.

Decision-making styles also vary. Some bosses are highly involved and need you to touch base frequently. Others prefer to delegate, so you should inform them about decisions you've already made. Do you know what your boss prefers?

How does your boss like to be kept in the loop about your work projects – by e-mail, voicemail, or face- to-face updates? If face-to-face, is a formal weekly meeting or a spontaneous discussion preferred?

Do you know if your boss requires the whole story, brief highlights, or a quick report followed up with in- depth documentation? You have to make sure you work around these preferences.

Rico's new boss wants to be copied on all e-mails, while his old boss just wanted a daily summary over coffee. Rico keeps forgetting to copy his boss on the e-mails, so his boss is not getting all the necessary information.

Rico, on the other hand, misses the feedback he used to get in informal meetings.

Rico now makes it a part of his routine to double check all e-mails at the end of the day. He also asked his boss for a weekly sit-down meeting so they can keep in better touch about the informal items Rico needs feedback on.

Mutual expectations

It's when you assume you know what the boss expects that trouble begins. Some bosses are explicit about what they want, but most are not. You need to clarify your mutual expectations.

Ultimately the burden falls on you to find out what your boss's expectations are and accommodate them. Expectations can range from what general kinds of problems your boss wants to know about to specifics such as project milestone dates.

Don't assume you know what your boss expects from you. Find out.

And work expectations go both ways. You need to communicate your own expectations and find out if they're realistic.

You might be in a situation where you expect open support or better communication from your boss, who may in turn have expectations of you that include more hours per week or a change in dress.

In Rico's case, his new boss is a real go-getter. In the first few weeks it becomes clear to Rico that he is expected to work additional hours on the weekend.

Rico is perfectly happy to do that in the short term, but lets the boss know that his family responsibilities won't allow him to work every weekend.

Together, they map out a balanced approach that fits both their needs.

Effective information flow

How much information a boss needs about what a subordinate is doing can depend on the boss's style, the situation, and the level of confidence the boss has.

However, administrative support professionals typically underestimate what their bosses need to know. Often, more information is needed than the subordinate would naturally supply.

Managing the flow of information is especially hard if you have a "good-news-only" boss who doesn't like to hear about problems. But for the good of the company, the boss, and yourself, tell your boss about failures as well as successes.

Rico's boss assumes that since he doesn't hear any complaints, morale is high. Rico, however, is aware of several unhappy employees but doesn't want his boss to think he's spreading rumors.

As a result, problems worsen before the boss notices, and Rico feels bad that he didn't speak up sooner. Rico now includes a segment on morale issues in his weekly report.

Dependability

Dependability and honesty are at the core of the trust needed to have a true partnership. Without trust, bosses feel compelled to check all of their subordinates' actions and can't delegate effectively.

As a trustworthy administrative support professional, don't make promises you can't keep, and don't shade the truth or play down difficult issues.

And you should certainly never be dishonest. Dishonestly undermines credibility and destroys confidence.

Rico is working on a documentation project for his new boss. Rico's tendency is to set and try to meet very optimistic deadlines, but he occasionally misses them.

The boss is used to a very structured approach with little flexibility, so this mismatch is causing the boss to feel like Rico's work can't be trusted.

To counter this, Rico decides to build in an extra day for each milestone deadline. He now doesn't miss any dates, and his boss can count on him delivering on time or early.

Good use of resources

Your boss has limited time and energy. Every request you make draws on resources, so you need to be selective and make good use of these assets.

So try not to waste your boss's time with trivial matters. Only draw on time and resources to meet the most important goals, whether they're yours, your boss's, or your organization's.

Because of the changeover in supervisors, Rico finds himself having to ask more questions and confirm policies and expectations. He's getting the feeling he's annoying his new boss.

He gets approval to ask only the highest-priority questions to minimize interruptions, and puts all others in a weekly e-mail. This way, the boss can clarify matters at his own convenience.

Rico also keeps a database of all the questions and answers, so he can create guidelines for himself when similar situations arise.

Question

What are the necessary elements for building and maintaining an effective partnership with your boss?

Options:

1. Having work styles that are attuned
2. Knowing what you and your boss expect from each other
3. Ensuring you present the right information in the way your boss prefers
4. Being reliable and trustworthy
5. Making the best use of time
6. Being honest if you and your boss are incompatible
7. Keeping your boss informed through processes that you know best

Answer:

Option 1: This is a correct option. Adapting your work style so it's compatible with your boss's is essential to building and maintaining an effective partnership.

Option 2: This is a correct option. Having mutual expectations builds trust and makes it clear what each of you need from the partnership.

Option 3: This is a correct option. For a partnership to happen, your boss needs to be able to depend on you for an accurate and substantive flow of information.

Option 4: This is a correct option. Dependability and honesty form the basis for a partnership, as they are at the core of trust.

Option 5: This is a correct option. Resources are always limited, so being able to make good use of time and assets helps build and maintain an effective partnership.

Option 6: This is an incorrect option. It's the administrative support professional's job to understand and accommodate a boss's preferred working style. You need to actively create compatible work styles.

Option 7: This is an incorrect option. In a true partnership, you and your boss will form compatible work styles. You need to be able to adapt to these styles, and not force accommodation on your boss.

You and your boss are interdependent, since if you don't accomplish your work, your boss won't be able to either. You need the information, perspective, experience, and support of your boss, and vice versa.

For a true partnership to take place between an administrative support professional and a boss, five crucial elements have to be in place. There must be compatible work styles, mutual expectations, an effective flow of information, dependability and honesty, and good use of resources.

DEALING WITH DIFFERENT MANAGEMENT STYLES

Dealing with different management styles

Identifying different management styles

Mimi is an administrative support professional whose previous manager – a relaxed boss who loved Mimi's work – got promoted. Mimi is now struggling. What's going on? Her new boss wants detailed written reports and structure. Mimi never had to research background information before a meeting, but now she keeps getting blindsided by unanticipated questions. And Mimi's new boss feels the meetings are inefficient. Why is her work style, which her old boss was so happy with, failing with her new boss?

As Mimi is finding out, different bosses have different management styles. And each style requires a different approach from administrative support professionals.

A large part of understanding your boss is being able to accommodate and adjust your work style to cope with your boss's style. Mimi had to learn to adapt to a more hands-on managerial style and identify the type of information her boss wanted.

Mimi now sends background reports and discussion agendas in advance. The result? Highly productive meetings, and even more innovative problem solving than she'd had with her previous boss.

Think about the bosses you've had in the past. Didn't they each have unique personalities? Some people are easy to read, and behave consistently under changing circumstances. Others are more challenging to work with. It's hard to label the different styles, since people don't fit into clearly defined types. But when under stress, the quirks that go along with people's dominant management styles become more evident.

You'll commonly encounter four different managerial styles in the workplace:

- The controller boss has a direct, authoritarian style.
- The manager with an open style values a democratic and team-oriented system.
- The bureaucrat is a boss who values processes and rules.
- The entrepreneur is a boss who's full of new ideas, energetic, and can be fun to work for.

Select each managerial style for more information.

The controller

Controllers value efficiency and productivity, and set clear, specific goals. They tend to micromanage their employees for maximum control. They don't tend to listen or take advice well.

The open manager

Open managers have general goals and don't give specific directions. They value relationships and enjoy chatting and getting together socially with employees.

The bureaucrat

Bureaucrats resist new and innovative ideas, preferring to base decisions on what's been done in the past. They have high respect for the chain of command within organizations.

The entrepreneur

Entrepreneurs are hard workers and often expect employees to go above and beyond their stated duties. They're visionaries who don't always use good business sense.

The descriptions of the four types of managers are exaggerated so you can clearly tell the differences between them. But remember that in real life, there are degrees of expression and overlap between styles. Your job as a partner to your boss isn't to change your boss's personality, but rather to understand it and be able to adjust your work to it.

Question

Consider this situation. One day, Ellen, the boss, came to the office excited about another new idea she had. Her staff gathered around as she described her plans. "I know it will take a lot of extra effort over the next while. We'll probably be in here over the next three weekends, but the payoffs are going to be huge!"

What do you think is Ellen's dominant style as a manager?

Options:

1. The controller
2. The open manager
3. The bureaucrat
4. The entrepreneur

Answer:

Option 1: This option is incorrect. If Ellen were a controller, she'd be using a direct, authoritarian style. Ellen uses an entrepreneur style; she's excited about her new plans and can't wait to get started.

Option 2: This option is incorrect. If Ellen's dominant style were that of an open manager, she'd ask what others think. Instead, Ellen's got an idea and can't wait to put it into practice, which is a characteristic of the entrepreneurial style of management.

Option 3: This option is incorrect. Ellen's dominant style is not that of a bureaucrat, with a strong reliance on following established patterns. She uses the entrepreneur style and can't wait to get started with her new project. She wants everyone else to be as excited as she is.

Option 4: This is the correct option. Ellen is excited about her new plans, can't wait to get started, and expects her staff to put in extra effort to execute her ideas. Ellen exhibits classic characteristics of a boss with an entrepreneurial style.

Adapting to the controller

When you can adapt to each of the various manager styles, you'll have the interpersonal skills required for a true partnership with almost any boss. But to do this, you'll need to learn the different strategies and approaches for dealing with each type.

Have you ever worked for a controller? Since this is one of the most common types of managers, maybe you've discovered techniques for adapting to this style. Overall, the best thing to do with controllers is to just let them be the boss. To avoid friction, be easygoing and flexible. Controllers don't appreciate resistance or making light of their authority. When you give a controller information or pitch a new idea, be brief and to the point.

Taku is an administrative support professional who works with a controller boss, Nils. Taku knows Nils sets great, clearly defined goals. Nils is also efficient, and helps the whole team be more productive.

But Nils insists on telling Taku what to do and how to do it in minute detail, even though Taku has excelled at his job for many years.

Nils is demanding and sometimes brutally honest – if he doesn't like something, he doesn't hesitate to say so. But Taku likes that he always knows where he stands, and overall, enjoys working with Nils.

Taku and Nils are preparing for an inspection by government authorities. The stakes are high, since they need official certification to remain in business. Follow along as Taku tries to adapt to Nils's work style.

Nils: Taku, I'd like you to go over the entire FDA "Investigations Operations Manual" so we'll know what the inspectors will be looking for.

Taku: Sure. I'll download the most recent version off the FDA web site.
Nils: Then you can draw up a checklist for the technicians to use as they prepare their workstations for the inspection.

Taku: Don't forget about the store rooms. Won't they want to see those?

Nils: I was just getting to that. Get Cindy to go through and make sure the bins are clearly labeled and things are clean.

Taku: I had another issue that needs discussion, but I'll wait until we get this inspection out of the way before we get together to talk about less-important issues.

Nils: Good. I appreciate that. Let's get to work.

Question

How do you think Taku did with his interaction with Nils?

Determine whether or not Taku's behaviors were helpful when dealing with a controller by matching the assessment to the behaviors.

Options:

A. Helpful behavior when dealing with a controlling boss

B. Less-helpful behavior when dealing with a controlling boss

Targets:

1. Taku's responses and questions were brief
2. Taku didn't complain about the tasks that Nils gave him
3. Taku gave Nils advanced warning about the future discussion
4. Taku reminded Nils about preparing the store rooms

Answer:

Brief questions and responses are particularly helpful when dealing with a controller. Taku understands that his boss prefers brevity.

Not complaining about the tasks that Nils gave him is a helpful behavior when dealing with a controller. Taku didn't resist the assignment. Nils would not have appreciated it if he had.

While postponing discussion of less-important details is a good move, giving Nils advanced warning about the future discussion is not particularly helpful when dealing with a controller. Taku needs to keep his questions and responses short.

Reminding Nils about preparing the store rooms is not particularly helpful. Nils is a micromanager and already had it in hand.

Taku was brief when he gave Nils information, and proved he was easygoing and flexible by not complaining. But he could improve his interactions with a controlling boss by staying on point and not interrupting the discussion by giving advanced warning of a future issue. He could also have just let Nils be the boss and not reminded him about the store rooms.

Question

Which are examples of appropriate responses to use with a controller boss?

Options:

1. Defer to your boss's authority and don't argue unnecessarily

2. Cooperate with the controller by letting the boss observe you while following instructions

3. Don't waste your boss's time unless you absolutely have to offer input

4. Try to discuss the problem you have with the boss's micromanagement

5. Miss some dates or make small inaccuracies in your work, so the boss has a credible opportunity to direct you

Answer:

Option 1: This option is correct. With a controlling boss, you have to take a back seat and yield to authority if you want to avoid unnecessary conflict.

Option 2: This option is correct. Be easygoing and flexible with controlling bosses, and go along with how they want you to do things.

Option 3: This option is correct. Be brief and to the point, and don't waste your boss's time unless your input is essential.

Option 4: This option is incorrect. Controlling bosses believe they're exerting just the right amount of control, not too much. Trying to change their minds will make it seem as though you're not letting them be the boss.

Option 5: This option is incorrect. Missing deadlines or being inaccurate will just make a controlling boss even more directive. You should always follow through on promises.

Adapting to the open manager

When your boss is a controller, you have to yield to authority. But what if your boss is a "softy" who has a hard time making tough decisions? And has an even harder time communicating unpopular decisions to staff members? To compensate for your boss's open style of management, you may be called upon to take a very different approach than for a controller.

Open managers are usually empowering and have great people skills, but these same characteristics can sometimes cause difficulties. Open managers need encouragement to be stronger leaders and to step outside their comfort zones. When working with an open manager, encourage your boss to take a strong leadership position and make undemocratic decisions when necessary, and be more specific with instructions and goals.

For example, Heather's boss, Rosa, has an open management style. Select each technique of adapting to an open manager for examples of how Heather encourages Rosa.

To take a strong leadership position

During a period of downtime for the company, Rosa lays off three designers. She finds it difficult since she is so close to her staff. Heather encourages her to do what she has to do and helps with the placement of the laid-off employees.

To make undemocratic decisions

Heather encourages Rosa to use her own decision-making skills and not unnecessarily seek the input of multiple team members. This increases Rosa's efficiency, since she now doesn't feel the need to include a large number of people in making decisions.

To be more specific

Heather asks Rosa for specifics when she gets an assignment. When setting production goals for the division, Heather works with Rosa to get down to specific, tangible goals, rather than staying at the general level.

Question

Which are examples of appropriate responses you could use with an open boss?

Options:

1. "I think you can make the call on this one on your own."
2. "Sometimes you have to make unpopular decisions."
3. "Does next week mean closer to Monday or Friday?"
4. "You really should consult the whole group on this issue."
5. "We need to look at the big picture."

Answer:

Option 1: This option is correct. An open boss has difficulty making decisions without a consensus, and needs encouragement. You may have to remind your boss about being the only person with the authority to make a decision.

Option 2: This option is correct. An open boss needs your encouragement to be a strong leader. Being supportive when unpopular decisions need to be made helps your boss move out of the comfort zone.

Option 3: This option is correct. An open boss usually needs to be more specific. Using questions that gently ask the boss for details helps provide essential data.

Option 4: This option is incorrect. Encouraging a group consensus will only exacerbate the tendency of an open boss to depend on subordinates for decision making.

Option 5: This option is incorrect. You have to guide an open boss into providing specific details, rather than remaining general. Big-picture views don't encourage your boss to be specific.

Adapting to the bureaucratic boss

Open managers are team-oriented, and put their trust in people more than rules. In contrast, bureaucratic bosses are procedure-oriented, and feel most secure using familiar practices and having thorough paper trails. As an example, consider Martina's boss, Tyrell. Tyrell uses a bureaucratic management style even though his organization has an informal, flattened structure.

Martina modified her own work style slightly to complement Tyrell's. This has strengthened their partnership over time.

Martina takes care to make sure that forms are filled out correctly and procedures are documented and followed. She respects the fact that Tyrell likes to stick to the "tried and true" ways of doing things.

To partner most effectively with a bureaucratic type of boss, administrative support professionals should use a couple of strategies:

- pay attention to paperwork, and follow rules and procedures, and
- be gentle, yet persistent, when introducing new ideas.

Follow along as Martina goes along with her bureaucratic boss, Tyrell, even when the red tape seems counterproductive to her.

Tyrell: Thanks for getting those forms filled out by this afternoon. I never have to worry about you leaving out anything important.

Martina: You're welcome!

Tyrell: I think it would be good to document the new procedure for locking up the office at night. I've noticed that computers aren't shut down and sometimes the lights are on overnight. Could you take care of that?

Martina: I could send out a reminder e-mail to the department. That would save time.

Tyrell: No. I really think we need to have the procedure in writing. We need to ensure that it's read and signed to show that the employees are taking responsibility for the daily office closure being done correctly.

Martina: Okay, Tyrell. I'll put that on my list of things to get done by the end of the week.

Another time, Martina was going over office expenses, trying to cut costs. She noticed printing costs had increased by 15%. She asked Tyrell if the team could submit weekly status reports electronically instead of in print to save time and money. Tyrell didn't like the idea at first, since he couldn't picture himself reading reports online. But after Martina repeated the benefits over the course of the week, he conceded.

Adapting to the entrepreneur

Bureaucratic bosses are all about following rules. But entrepreneurial bosses are looser, and sometime lose sight of the rules completely while following their vision. You can easily find entrepreneurs in management. In technology industries, entrepreneurs with engineering or computer backgrounds lead many major companies. Entrepreneurs have drive and determination, which takes these bosses to the top. But it can also make them somewhat difficult to partner with.

Entrepreneurs need administrative support personnel who can complement their management style by offering sound human resource and business practices. When working with an entrepreneur, you'll need to enforce your personal limits on how much you will give to the job. You should act as the voice of reason to moderate your boss's new ideas, and develop strong business principles. Using these techniques, you'll balance your boss's strengths.

See each technique for more information about dealing with an entrepreneur boss.

Enforce personal limits

Entrepreneur bosses may expect you to put in the same long hours and degree of effort that they do. Set and enforce your personal limits firmly, yet politely.

Act as the voice of reason

Entrepreneur bosses are full of ideas for trying new things. Play devil's advocate. Act as the voice of reason by making sure new schemes are viable. Of course, let your boss know what you're doing so that you don't come across as negative and overly critical.

Develop strong business principles

By developing strong business principles, you can help keep entrepreneurs grounded in the realities of your industry. Take business courses, and discuss your role as the "business-minded" one with your boss so you know your opinion will be welcomed.

Bhadrak works as an executive assistant at a large computer company. His boss, Kyra, is an entrepreneurial manager. Kyra started the company just ten years ago and has seen it grow to become one of the largest in the region. Bhadrak helps Kyra by keeping her grounded.

See each technique for an example of how Bhadrak sets limits, plays devil's advocate, and helps on the business side of the operation.

Enforce personal limits

At first, Kyra expected Bhadrak to stay at work until the tasks she'd given him for the day were done. Bhadrak had to make it clear that he could stay until 6:00 p.m. when really necessary, but on a normal day, he would be going home at 5:00 p.m.

Act as the voice of reason

Kyra comes up with some pretty far-fetched ideas. Once, she had an idea for a computer application that would allow users to star in their own online TV show. Bhadrak thought it was a great idea, but put forward arguments against it to test the validity of the proposition. Kyra ended up understanding how difficult and costly it would be to design.

Develop strong business principles

Bhadrak learned how to do elementary cost estimates using function point analysis, a cost estimating model frequently used in the software industry. This allowed him to better judge the viability of Kyra's visions.

Any experienced admin support professional could tell you that a boss can exhibit characteristics of two management styles at a time. For example, do you feel that you work for a "bureaucratic controller" or perhaps an "open entrepreneur?" Many combinations are possible. You may feel that your boss doesn't fall clearly into any one category. However, review how your boss behaves when the pressure is on, and take that style as your guide.

Question

Match the type of boss to the examples of behaviors you could use to best adapt to each boss's style. Not all the behaviors have a match.

Options:

A. The bureaucrat

B. The entrepreneur

Targets:

1. Make sure you "cross your t's and dot your i's"
2. Be the partner with the good "business head"
3. Be firm with your boss and offer good advice and criticism
4. Use courtesy with persuasion when suggesting new ways to do things
5. Politely define how much overtime you can work
6. Let your boss be the boss unless you absolutely have to offer input

Answer:

A bureaucratic boss thrives in an environment of paperwork, rules, and procedures. Paying attention to particulars works best for this boss.

Developing strong business principles is appropriate for dealing with the entrepreneurial boss. Entrepreneurs sometimes don't pay attention to detail.

Being firm and offering good advice is a good way to act as the voice of reason for an entrepreneurial boss. You can do your boss a big favor by making sure new schemes are viable.

Using courtesy with persuasion is a way of being gentle, yet persistent when introducing new ideas. This technique will appeal to a boss with a bureaucratic style.

You need to be definite about extra hours and other beyond-the-call-of-duty requests. Setting and enforcing personal limits is an effective technique to use with an entrepreneurial boss.

Actually, this suggestion is appropriate for dealing with the controlling boss. With a controlling boss, you have to take a back seat and yield to authority if you want to avoid unnecessary conflict.

As an administrative support professional, you'll work with different types of bosses. Being able to recognize appropriate responses for dealing with bosses exhibiting particular management styles – whether they're controllers, open managers, bureaucrats, or entrepreneurs – will allow you to truly partner with them.

For the controller boss, you should let the boss be the boss, be flexible, and be brief. For the open manager, encourage the boss to take a strong leadership position, make undemocratic decisions, and be specific. The bureaucrat needs you to follow procedures and be gentle yet persistent when introducing new ideas. And with an entrepreneurial boss, enforce personal limits, act as the voice of reason, and develop strong business principles.

SUCCESSFULLY HANDLE A CONFRONTATION WITH YOUR BOSS

Successfully handle a confrontation with your boss

Determining if confrontation is needed

Conflict is inevitable. It happens whenever people with different points of view work together to achieve common goals. But conflict can be a healthy thing in your relationship with your boss if it's handled correctly. The key to doing so lies in knowing when it's appropriate to confront your boss and in conducting yourself properly during a confrontation.

Considerations when determining if you should confront your boss:

Having some criteria can be helpful when deciding whether a confrontation with your boss is worthwhile. You don't want to argue with your boss about unimportant things or get involved in conflict that doesn't directly involve you.

When deciding whether or not to confront, ask yourself these questions:

– Will the problem persist if I don't deal with it?

– Would I be acting in the best interest of others?

– Is a confrontation over this matter likely to strengthen our partnership?

When a potential conflict situation arises, you should ask yourself the three specific questions about each area to help determine when to address an issue and when to let it pass.

Answering "yes" to any one of the questions means you have a legitimate reason to confront. But just one reason alone will probably not justify the effort and risk to your work relationship of a confrontation. If you can answer "yes" to two or three of them, you have a strong case for confronting.

Imagine you're an administrative support professional at a manufacturing company. One day as you go to the copy machine, you hear your boss, Ian, say something derogatory about you. He says, "Thanks for doing this. My assistant isn't very good at event planning."

It's bothering you, and you would really like to ask your boss how he could say such a thing.

Question

Making the decision to confront isn't always easy. You're trying to decide whether to ask about what you overheard.

Do you think you'd be justified in confronting Ian in this situation?

Options:

1. Yes, very justified
2. Yes, quite justified
3. Not quite justified
4. Not at all justified

Answer:

Option 1: If you answered "yes" to all three questions, you'd be very justified in confronting the boss. In this situation, not all of the questions could result in "yes" answers.

Option 2: Answering "yes" to two questions means you're quite justified in confronting your boss over this situation. In this case, two questions might be answered with a "yes."

Option 3: If you answered "yes" to one of the three questions, you probably have a legitimate issue, but one reason isn't enough justification to confront. In this situation, two questions could have a "yes" answer.

Option 4: If you answered "no" to all three questions, you wouldn't be at all justified in confronting your boss. In this case, two questions could be answered with a "yes."

In this situation, you're quite justified in talking to Ian. You don't want him thinking you're not good at one of your functions, and this problem will persist if you don't deal with it. While it doesn't reflect well on you or Ian if he makes disparaging remarks about you, you're really acting in your own interest. It's certainly in the best interest of your relationship to fix the problem, so confronting your boss is the right thing to do.

Handling a confrontation

Suppose that after going though the decision-making process, you determine that you need to confront your boss. Or perhaps your boss decides to confront you about something. Conducting yourself properly during a conflict with your boss is vital to the success of your partnership. In confrontations, you need to be assertive, not aggressive or passive.

Communicating assertively helps you reduce mistakes and inefficiencies caused by misunderstandings, motivate others, and get the desired result.

You may think you're being assertive, but you need to pay attention to how others interpret your communication style, as well.

Major differences exist between the three styles of communication:

- Being passive means you don't engage the other person, you withdraw, and you allow others to choose and make decisions for you. Others achieve their goals at your expense. Passive people are often indirect, and feel anxious, ignored, helpless, or manipulated.
- Being aggressive means you go on the offensive, attacking people along with issues. Aggressive people are ruled by emotions and lose control. They achieve their goals at the expense of others. Direct and forceful, they demand their own way. Aggressive people feel righteous and controlling, while later they often feel guilt.
- Being assertive means you let others know your ideas and feelings, while respecting their feelings. Assertive people are prepared to speak up about results or problems they've encountered beyond their control. They're self-respecting, self-expressive, and straightforward. They achieve their goals at no one's expense.

Consider this situation. Suppose you have a boss, Yvette, who asks you to run a personal errand for her on your lunch break. You don't have the time, and you don't want to. Select the communication styles for examples of how you might respond.

Passive

A passive response would be to cut short your lunch and run the errand. You avoid immediate conflict, but there's a consequence. Passivity often provokes you to anger and resentment because you don't express your true feelings.

Aggressive

An aggressive response would be to tell Yvette, "No, I won't do it, you're being presumptuous. You always ask me to do stuff for you and I end up canceling my plans. And besides, your work already takes up too much of my time." While these things may reflect how you truly feel, your aggressive response will probably anger your boss.

Assertive

An assertive answer is honest and direct, but not disrespectful. You could say "No, I'm sorry I can't do that today. If you need me to help you out in the future, let me know the day before so I can fit it into my schedule. I also need you to work with me to define the limits of my responsibilities." Such assertive behavior allows you to express needs, thoughts, and feelings, and it produces the desired results.

Learning three straightforward techniques will help you handle a confrontation with your boss in a manner that avoids passivity and aggression. To confront your boss assertively, focus on the issue, not the person. Acknowledge your contribution to the problem in a realistic way, without being meek or putting undue blame on yourself. And finally, close any confrontation on a good note.

The first technique, focusing on the issue, will allow you to be honest with your boss about how you feel without launching a personal attack.

Using this technique allows negative emotions, such as anger or frustration, to energize you, and spur you to action without controlling you.

Consider this situation. One of your coworkers, Joe, has been unfairly passed over for a promotion. You've asked yourself the three questions, and believe the problem will persist if it's not addressed, that discussing it would be acting in the best interest of yourself and others, and that a confrontation over the matter could strengthen your partnership with your boss by clarifying expectations.

Question

What do you think would be the assertive way to raise the issue of Joe's promotion with your boss?

Options:

1. "I think Joe was in line for that position."
2. "You're being really unfair to Joe."
3. "Some people are unhappy about it, but I think you made a good choice with the promotion."

Answer:

Option 1: This is the correct option. With an assertive response that focuses on the issue, you're targeting the perceived injustice of the situation.

Option 2: This is an incorrect option. Immediately going on the attack is focusing on your boss's character, not the issue. This is an aggressive response, not an assertive one.

Option 3: This is an incorrect option. Being indirect is a passive way to address the issue, not an assertive way.

Now consider Mario's situation. He just learned that his boss Amrit took back control of a project that she said he could head up. Mario takes a deep breath before he enters Amrit's office. Follow along as he confronts his boss.

Mario: Amrit, can you explain something I'm finding frustrating? I don't understand why I'm not in charge of the editorial project for the new client.

Amrit: Well, after I reviewed the scope of the project, I felt that it would be better if I took it over.

Mario: What aspects of the scope did you feel were beyond my abilities?

Amrit: This project is going to require a lot of detailed documentation. You'd have to create style guides and keep to rigid standards. Frankly,

Mario, I just don't feel comfortable with your level of knowledge in that area.

Mario: That may be, but I'm sure we could've worked something out together. I would really appreciate it if, in the future, we could discuss issues like this before you make decisions that affect me.

Question

Consider Mario's discussion with Amrit. Did he properly handle the confrontation?

Options:

1. Yes
2. No

Answer:

Mario kept the focus on the issue. He didn't personally attack Amrit's character, and only discussed Amrit's decision-making process.

The second technique in handling a confrontation with your boss is to acknowledge your contribution to the problem. This is especially useful if you are the one who is being confronted about something you've done. You'll be surprised at how this simple act of humility can disarm a potentially damaging situation. After all, the goal is to improve the relationship with your boss, not destroy it.

When you're the person being confronted, the most natural response is to become defensive. If your boss confronts you, be open-minded about the criticism. Maybe there's some truth in it. Admitting responsibility will help you strengthen your relationship.

When you're the one confronting your boss, you may ask, "Why should I admit blame when I'm the one challenging my boss about something?" While it won't always apply, carefully consider whether the problem has stemmed from any oversight, error, or lack of communication on your part.

The final technique for handling confrontation in an assertive manner can be summed up in a wise saying: "Don't let the sun go down on your anger." This is crucial for maintaining a healthy relationship with your boss. Make sure you stick with the discussion until you both feel that the problem is resolved. Do whatever you can to close the confrontation on a good note.

Remember Mario and Amrit's confrontation? Follow along again as Mario now makes an effort to accept some responsibility for the problem and close the meeting positively.

Mario: I'm not pleased with how this was handled. But I should have told you about my plans to get Kelly to help me out with the parts that I couldn't do myself.

Amrit: Yes. I didn't realize that you were going to bring someone else in. All I could see was the importance of getting the style guide and standards to the client right away and for the documents to be as complete as possible.

Mario: Well, I'm glad we talked about this. I feel better than I did. We'll just know to communicate a little better the next time we run into something like this.

Amrit: Yes. I'm glad you came to see me about this, too. Now I know you're really on top of things.

Mario acknowledged his contribution to the problem by admitting to Amrit that he should have informed her about his plan to get help. He ended the confrontation on a positive note as well, by saying that he feels better after the discussion and not reminding Amrit about how frustrated he was with her.

Assertive people have self-respect, can express themselves clearly, and are straightforward. You needed all those traits to handle the confrontation with Ian appropriately so you could resolve the problem. During a confrontation like this, you need to keep your focus on the issue, accept the part you play in the problem, and end the discussion on a good note. Using these techniques, you can have a successful encounter that strengthens your relationship with your boss.

Make sure that the partnership between you and your boss continues to grow by correctly managing conflicts when they arise.

If you determine that a confrontation is justified, the techniques you should use are to focus on the issue, not the person; acknowledge your contribution to the problem; and close any confrontation on a good note.

CHAPTER IV - INTERACTING WITH OTHERS

CHAPTER IV - Interacting with Others

This chapter is designed to help you handle interactions more effectively. Whether it's interacting with your boss, a client, or a coworker, you'll learn how to be a more supportive player.

The book also provides guidelines for asking for help, an interaction you'll inevitably encounter in your career as an administrative professional. You'll also learn how to handle criticism in the workplace. The course gives you guidelines on taking criticism well and challenging unfair criticism appropriately.

When you learn how to handle the various interactions you're likely to encounter, you'll have acquired an important skill set for succeeding in the workplace. These skills will help you meet your goals, as well as your company's and your boss's goals. You'll improve your reputation as a team player and improve your relationships throughout the organization.

HOW TO BE A SUPPORTIVE COLLEAGUE

How to be a supportive colleague

Benefits of being supportive

Kim is an executive assistant at a car manufacturing company. As an administrative support professional, her day is spent interacting with her boss, customers, other employees within and outside her department, upper management, as well as computer and office equipment sales and service representatives. She's achieved her position by knowing how to interact with different people and by being known as a supportive team player.

You, like Kim, can be a supportive member of your company. This means keeping your boss's and your company's goals in mind and supporting others to achieve them.

Being supportive means being positive about others' contributions, giving credit where it's due, and avoiding attempts to "win" or look good at the expense of others.

Supportive team members are quick to share information and ideas, and are open to the ideas and feedback of others.

When you and others are supportive in these ways, you create a team that has several important characteristics:

- Effective teams have a high level of trust among team members and toward the leader. When team members support one another, politics is kept to a minimum. When trust is high, criticisms are good natured and constructive, and communication is open. No one criticizes anyone else behind their backs.
- Supportive teams have a high degree of respect among members, and for the boss. In addition to respecting your teammates, you must earn their respect to be effective. This means proving you can contribute on par with other team members.

- In a highly effective team, there is a sense of unity. The team is like a family, with a sense of belonging and strong loyalty among teammates and to the boss. The team tends to stick together through organizational changes and is resistant to outside pressures.
- On supportive teams, members communicate openly, directly, and often. Mutual respect and trust among members create a "safe" environment for speaking up about problems, or presenting new ideas. Everyone assumes the best intentions, so disagreement and debates are good natured, relaxed, and a healthy part of a team's communication.
- Supportive teams have a general lack of selfishness. Team members know that from time to time some of their coworkers will be in the spotlight, but eventually everyone wins if the team wins. Supportive members will often step out of the spotlight and refocus the attention on others.

Question

Lack of selfishness is important in your role as an administrative professional.

When it comes to work, how good are you at leaving your ego behind? Options:

1. Not very good
2. Good
3. Very good

Answer:

Option 1: Keeping your ego out of your work is important if you want to be more supportive in the workplace. Striving for personal credit or gain can interfere with getting the job done, in which case you aren't being supportive of your boss's goals and, ultimately, those of the company.

Option 2: When you leave your ego behind, you avoid getting bogged down by trying to meet your own needs. You can focus on what's good for the team and what helps advance your boss's goals. In the end, you'll be more productive.

Option 3: Leaving your ego behind helps you to be more supportive and productive in the workplace. As a more supportive member of your boss's team, you'll be better able to meet not only your boss's goals, but also your own goals of being an effective administrative professional.

So leaving your ego behind benefits you by enabling you to focus on important goals and therefore be more productive. Being supportive can benefit you in other ways too.

How being supportive benefits your relationships:

When your teammates and your boss know they can count on you to be supportive, they'll be supportive in return. You'll benefit because mutual trust increases, which in turn enhances your work relationships.

So, two benefits of being supportive are that it helps you meet important goals and builds trust, and therefore improves your relationships with others in the office.

But there's another benefit you'll receive by being supportive – it gets you recognized as a strong team player. As a result, you may find that you're much in demand when new projects or business opportunities arise.

Question

How can you benefit from being a supportive member of your organization?

Options:

1. You'll accomplish your goals and be more productive
2. You'll be recognized as a strong team player
3. Your workload will be reduced because your teammates will be supportive in return
4. Your relationships within the organization will improve
5. You'll come to be recognized as the driving force behind the team's success

Answer:

Option 1: This option is correct. When you're a supportive member of your organization, you increase your personal power – people trust you and in turn are supportive of you. This improves your ability to accomplish your goals and be more productive. In addition, being supportive means leaving your ego behind. This helps you focus on goals that are important to you, your boss, and your company.

Option 2: This option is correct. When you're supportive, your teammates and your boss will know they can trust you to be a strong team player. When this happens, leaders will seek you out for new projects.

Option 3: This is an incorrect option. While teammates may respond in kind, this won't reduce your workload. You may find that getting things done is easier, but you still have your own tasks and goals to accomplish.

Option 4: This option is correct. When you're a supportive member of your organization, relationships are enhanced because people trust you and are supportive in return.

Option 5: This is an incorrect option. While others may come to value you highly, your job is supporting others, particularly your boss. Part of being an administrative professional is leaving your ego behind so that you can better help to accomplish your boss's goals, as well as your own.

Strategies for being supportive

Administrative support professionals provide information, guide visitors and callers to the right person, conduct interviews, delegate tasks, and negotiate solutions. Being an outstanding administrative support professional doesn't come from thinking only of yourself. It comes from working together with colleagues and managers as a team to get the job done.

As an administrative support professional, being supportive of your colleagues, your manager, and your team is at the core of your job. You will find specific ways of being supportive, depending on the situations you face. But routinely following four general strategies can help make you a truly supportive member of your company team. These strategies are leave your ego behind, cooperate with your boss and the team you work with, be open to new ideas, and give a little extra from time to time.

The first strategy that will help you be more supportive is to remember to leave your ego behind when dealing with other team members.

You should certainly accept praise for your efforts, but also remember to share praise with teammates and coworkers when they deserve it.

If your boss praises a job well done, you should publicly acknowledge others who helped you accomplish the job.

Another strategy for being supportive is to cooperate with your boss and the team you work with. This means more than just following orders and doing a good job with the tasks you've been assigned.

A supportive administrative professional ensures the boss and team are informed and up to date about relevant issues. As new issues arise, your boss needs to know about them sooner rather than later.

You must work with your boss's team to advance the company's goals and to ensure your boss has what is needed to succeed.

Being open to new ideas also helps you be a more supportive member of the team. You shouldn't reject other people's suggestions without fair consideration. You must keep in mind that things don't always have to be done the same way.

An example can illustrate the strategies of cooperating with the boss and team, and being open to new ideas. Gerard is an administrative professional for a transportation company. He has been assigned to represent administrative support personnel on a committee formed to discuss changes to the company's HR policies.

Select each of the strategies that Gerard employed for more information.

Cooperating with boss and team

Part of Gerard's job is to work with his colleagues in administrative support to develop a prioritized list of job benefits and identify alternative options for benefit packages.

Gerard must also provide his boss, the committee leader, with the important information she needs. As each new idea is proposed, Gerard sends her an e-mail to ensure she is kept up to date.

Being open to new ideas

Gerard was originally in favor of changing the existing monthly bonus plan to a yearly one. But Carla, another administrative support professional, proposed an entirely different program based on a variety of criteria.

Gerard initially considered Carla's program too complex, but he presented it fairly to his boss, and in doing so, came to understand and approve of Carla's suggestion.

By effectively supporting his boss and by keeping an open mind, Gerard has built a reputation as a team player. He is now in demand and often invited to participate in new projects. He is becoming much more visible within the organization.

Another way of showing that you're a supportive member of the company team is to give a little extra. You should always consider whether there is something else you could do to make an even greater contribution to the team, your boss, or the company – even if this means taking on more than your usual responsibilities.

For example, what if your boss asks you to review a process to try to make it more efficient, and in the course of your work, you find another administrative process that could be improved?

You could be proactive and provide a high-level review of that process as well.

Some administrative professionals may work extra hours to help out. For example, Neil is an administrative support professional for the director of admissions at a university. An unusually large number of applications need to be reviewed in time for the next semester enrollment, and his manager, Bella, is under a lot of pressure. Neil goes the extra mile by volunteering to work extra hours over the next few weeks to help Bella complete the work.

Question 1 of 2

Your boss has praised you for a template you prepared for tracking the progress of accepted manuscripts. But he cannot discuss it further with you. He is under pressure to finish reviewing several manuscripts before the next meeting with the publisher, as well as finish sending rejection letters.

How can you demonstrate that you're a supportive member of the team in this situation?

Options:

1. Thank your boss and also mention that the technical support team was very helpful in providing tracking software

2. Offer to help with the rejection letters after hours on Friday

3. Empathize with your boss about the extra work he has and tell him you'll stay out of his way

4. Tell your boss you know you did a great job on template and that it required some help from the technical team, but not much

Answer:

Option 1: This is a correct option. Although you should accept praise graciously, as a supportive team member, you must set your ego aside and share the credit.

Option 2: This is a correct option. Giving a little extra, such as going beyond your required duties, shows you support your boss and the whole team.

Option 3: This is an incorrect option. To be supportive, it's important to find ways to give a little extra. Perhaps you could find time on your lunch hour or after work.

Option 4: This is an incorrect option. You should accept the praise and, if appropriate, share it with specific team members. This statement just diffuses and dilutes the praise.

Question 2 of 2

Your boss asks you to take a look at some ideas that have been submitted by a few of your colleagues in administrative support.

Which actions reflect the use of strategies for being a supportive team member?

Options:

1. You examine your colleagues' ideas and try to fairly evaluate their usefulness

2. You work with a colleague to develop one of his ideas more fully because it may be the best answer

to the boss's problem

3. You decide not to check out the improvement ideas because you know the present process works

fine for you

4. You go over the ideas but don't take it any further than that until your boss tells you to

Answer:

Option 1: This is a correct option. As an administrative professional, being open to new ideas is important to demonstrate that the good of the team comes first.

Option 2: This is a correct option. It's important to cooperate with your colleagues and your boss to help achieve your boss's goals.

Option 3: This is an incorrect option. You need to stay open to new ideas in order to be a supportive member of your boss's team. If you refuse to consider the ideas, others may be offended and think you're being unfairly judgmental.

Option 4: This is an incorrect option. You support your boss and your teammates when you're proactive and take on a little extra.

Unlike some other professions, excelling as an administrative professional is not about getting ahead of the pack. It's about supporting and facilitating your team's progress.

Being supportive improves your ability to get things done. Your work relationships are enhanced because you work more effectively with the people around you. You also benefit by being recognized as a strong team player.

You can use the four important strategies for being a supportive colleague and team member to help you achieve this. You must leave your ego behind, cooperate with your boss and your coworkers, remain open to new ideas, and always remember to give a little extra.

HOW TO EFFECTIVELY ASK FOR HELP

How to effectively ask for help

How to ask for help

As an administrative support professional, Jasmine has a variety of duties. She takes calls, receives visitors, sets her boss's schedule, maintains the file system, does research, and arranges for office maintenance and repair. At her boss's request, she's also helping HR prepare for the annual company meeting on Thursday. This morning her computer crashed and an important database file she was working with was lost. How can she re-create the database in two days so it's ready for Thursday's meeting?

Sometimes, as an administrative professional, you need to ask for help. At other times, you may be asked to help someone else. If you demonstrate you're willing to help when needed, you'll usually find that others will be ready and willing to assist you as well.

The types of assistance you may need will vary. You may need to ask a coworker to look after the phones when you have to be out of the office.

Or you may have a colleague skilled at graphics and layout who can help you with a presentation.

Whatever the task you need done, it's important to approach the process of asking for help in the right way. Follow these three steps when you ask for help: think about and determine exactly what you need, make your request, and then follow up with the person you asked the favor of.

See each of the three steps for more information about asking for help.

Determine exactly what you need

Before you approach the person you're going to ask for help, you need to consider the specifics of the task that you need done. Getting the person to focus on the right things will save time and effort and avoid misunderstanding. Consider any limits, boundaries, standards, and deadlines that might apply.

Make your request

Once you know exactly what you need, you're ready to make your request. Let people know why you need their help, exactly what you need them to do, and when you need the task completed.

Follow up

The third step for asking for help is to follow up to make sure everything is going well and to see if the person is having any problems you can help with. For this step, you check in to make sure that your instructions have been clear enough and whether the person has everything needed. At the same time, you can determine if what you've requested will be ready by your deadline.

Determine what you need

Carefully determining exactly what you need in advance goes a long way to ensuring you eventually get what you want. Before you approach a colleague and ask for help, you need to think about what specific actions will do you the most good.

Do you want someone to come by and help you with the promotion campaign, stuff 500 envelopes with flyers, design a logo for the campaign, or answer telephones for three hours?

Being clear in your head about what actions you need not only helps to ensure you get exactly what you need, it helps you clarify the scope and nature of the activity for the person you're asking.

For example, if you ask someone for help with a promotions campaign, the person may wonder what this means exactly. And this person may have negative feelings about it, thinking something along the lines of "I don't know much about promotions. Will I have to go out into the public? I'm not sure I want to help." If instead you ask for help stuffing 500 flyers into envelopes, the person understands exactly what's involved and may be more receptive to helping out.

The point of asking for help is to accomplish what you need to. So to ensure that's what happens, think about the key elements of the task:

- Consider the boundaries and scope of what you need. What exactly do you want the other person to do? Do you want this person to focus on one aspect of a task more than another? If you determine the limits now, you will save wasted work and eliminate the possibility of misunderstanding later.
- Also consider what standards the task has to meet. If you assume people share your standards, you'll probably be disappointed much of the time. For example, for a finished document, decide if it matters whether it's in a particular font, font size, or format, or whether it's printed on a particular type of paper.

- Think about when the task needs to be completed. If you need figures compiled by Thursday so that you have time to go over them for the Friday meeting, you need to determine that now. If you simply ask a colleague for help preparing the figures for Friday's meeting, you may not receive them in time to review before the deadline.

In this example of determining what's needed, Otto is an administrative support professional preparing a proposal for reorganizing the office workflow. Before asking for Sheila's help, he considers what he really needs. He sets boundaries by asking Sheila to review the document for grammar and style issues only. Facts and figures will be checked in a separate review. Otto then recalls that he'll need Sheila to use the company style guide as her standard and decides to ask her to finish her review by next Tuesday.

Question

Chuck, an administrative support professional, has been tasked with arranging travel for his boss to the company's annual convention. His current duties have him tied up, so he asks a colleague for some help.

What should Chuck consider before he asks for help?

Options:

1. What his boss's requirements are with regard to type of transportation and accommodation
2. Whether his colleague will need to handle everything or just booking the flight, hotel, and rental car
3. How soon he needs the colleague to get back to him with confirmed reservations
4. What payment the person will need for helping out
5. How to phrase his request so his colleague doesn't get a sense of how much work is involved

Answer:

Option 1: This is a correct option. When determining specifically what you need a person to do, you have to consider any standards the person must apply to do the task.

Option 2: This is a correct option. Thinking about the boundaries of your request is important to ensure you can clearly state the nature and scope of your need.

Option 3: This is a correct option. You must consider any deadlines the person helping you must meet. You will want travel confirmations in time to allow other plans to move forward.

Option 4: This is an incorrect option. Typically, you don't pay someone for helping you. If you're supportive of others, they'll be supportive of you.

And likewise, when people help you out, you'll likely come to their aid when they need you.

Option 5: This is an incorrect option. Rather than trying to cover up the amount of work you're asking for, you should be considering how to be clear about what exactly needs to be done.

Make your request

After you've considered all the angles and determined specifically what you need, your next step is to communicate this information effectively when you make your request. To do this, you explain to your colleague why you need the task done, be specific about what you want, and identify the deadline that must be met.

People are more likely to help you when you explain why you need their help.

If, for example, you need someone to answer your phone for a few hours, what do you say? If you don't explain why you need the help, the person may wonder whether you're taking an extended lunch for some reason.

If, instead, you explain that your boss asked you to take a CPR class that is given only during work hours, there would be no doubts that asking for help was a reasonable request.

When making your request, be specific about what you want. If you ask someone to "work on a reorganization project" with you, that person will have no sense of what the job entails, how difficult it will be, or whether or not she has the skills to accomplish the task for you. But if you specifically ask the person to "reorganize and alphabetize 50 personnel files for 2 hours on Friday morning," then the nature and scope of what you need is clearly understood. As a result, she may be more willing to help.

If you want the work done on time, it's also crucial to identify the deadline or time frame for the person you're asking help of.

Specifying the deadline will provide the information required for the individual to plan and schedule, and help ensure that the work is completed early enough to truly be of help to you.

If you leave the deadline vague or unspoken, the person may not see the need to start early enough to finish on time.

Leah is an administrative professional. She is working on an urgent project for her boss to update the company handbook. Because of that project, she can't attend the weekly budget meeting where she regularly acts as recording secretary.

Leah asks her colleague, Mark, for assistance.

She says "Mark, can you please cover for me as recording secretary for the two-hour budget meeting on Friday at 2 p.m.? I have a conflicting meeting for the handbook project. I will need the minutes of the meeting on my desk by 5 p.m. Is this something you could fit in?"

Leah lets Mark know when the job needs to be finished, why she needs his help, and exactly what she needs him to do.

Question

Chuck, the administrative professional, is about to approach the colleague he selected to help him with making travel arrangements.

Which is the most effective way for Chuck to ask for help?

Options:

1. Chuck should explain to his colleague that normally he would have time to make these arrangements himself, but he currently has all the work he can handle keeping up with compiling the end-of-year statistics

2. Chuck should ask his colleague to book an aisle seat on a flight leaving Monday and returning Thursday, as well as a nonsmoking hotel room and a mid-sized rental car for the corresponding time period

3. Chuck should explain that he needs all three reservations confirmed by tomorrow at 10:00 a.m.

4. Chuck should be succinct and simply state that he needs some help booking travel arrangements for his boss and that he'll return the favor at a later date

5. Chuck should specifically ask his colleague to book the flight, hotel, and rental car but avoid showing weakness by explaining why he needs the help

Answer:

Option 1: This is a correct option. People are more likely to help you when you explain why you need their help. They'll understand that you have a valid need.

Option 2: This is a correct option. Chuck needs to be specific about what he wants his colleague to do for him.

Option 3: This is a correct option. Chuck should identify the deadline for his colleague so that there's no misunderstanding and arrangements are made in due time.

Option 4: This is an incorrect option. When making a request, Chuck should be specific and provide a deadline. Vaguely stating what he needs will make the nature and scope of his request unclear.

Option 5: This is an incorrect option. Chuck no doubt has good reasons for asking for help. Explaining these reasons as he makes his request is important.

Follow up

The third step in asking for help from a colleague is to follow up on the request. But you don't follow up just to check up on the person.

You also do it to ensure your colleague has what's needed, and that everything is on track and on schedule.

You follow up to be supportive and to ensure that there is no wasted effort. You want to avoid giving an impression of mistrust or doubt about abilities. For example, you shouldn't ask your boss to check up on the person and you don't want to hover over your colleague. Both actions can put added pressure on the individual.

An administrative professional, Dominique, asked a coworker to compile figures on the effects of vacation scheduling on performance. Although the deadline isn't until tomorrow, Dominique gives her coworker a quick call today to see how the work is coming along and whether there's anything Dominique can do to help. During the conversation, it comes out that the colleague was unaware that certain information was vital. Fortunately, Dominique had called in plenty of time for him to incorporate the data before the deadline.

Question

Chuck, the administrative professional asking help of a colleague in booking travel for his boss, needs to make sure his colleague takes care of booking his boss's flight, hotel room, and rental car by 10:00 a.m. tomorrow.

How should Chuck ensure that the task is dealt with properly?

Options:

1. Check in with his colleague every other hour to find out if everything is booked yet

2. Call the colleague before the end of the day to find out if Chuck can help with any problems or issues

3. Have his boss check with the colleague to ensure that the job gets done right

Answer:

Option 1: This is an incorrect option. Chuck specified the deadline as tomorrow at 10:00 a.m. Checking in every other hour may make his colleague feel like Chuck is hovering.

Option 2: This is the correct option. Checking in prior to the deadline to offer support serves to avoid problems and wasted work, and establishes that the work is on track for the deadline.

Option 3: This is an incorrect option. Chuck shouldn't involve his boss or put pressure on the person he has asked for help. He should check in prior to the deadline and offer support.

You follow three steps to successfully ask for help from a colleague. You need to consider and determine exactly what you need, make your request, and follow up properly with the person you asked help of to ensure successful and timely completion of the task.

Actions related to these steps include deciding and specifying the boundaries, standards, and deadline; communicating the reasons for the help request; and following up on the request to offer support and ensure successful completion.

TECHNIQUES TO DEAL WITH CRITICISM

Techniques to deal with criticism

Dealing with criticism

Maya, an administrative support professional, submitted a proposal for new office purchases to the Procurement Department. The person in charge, Warren, paid a visit to her desk to talk to her about the submission. He pointed out several errors, including some style and grammar issues. The criticism was constructive and given in a friendly way, and Maya should have no trouble making the fixes and resubmitting the proposal in plenty of time.

Receiving criticism

When someone criticizes you, you may feel bad – no matter how well intentioned the criticism is or how much you agree with the person's comments.

A common first reaction to criticism is defensiveness, and sometimes you may even feel angry. This is normal. But if you can set aside those emotions and deal constructively with criticism – for example, by asking for suggestions on how to develop a solution – you'll be more productive in your job. Feeling resentful about criticism will have a negative effect on how you do your job.

It's inevitable that you will receive criticism during your career. And an administrative support professional may be likelier than most to face criticism due to the number and variety of people and situations encountered in the course of a day. Learning to handle criticism is an important skill for succeeding in the workplace, and three techniques can help you to deal constructively with criticism. To make it a positive experience, you should listen actively, assess whether to challenge the criticism, and ask for suggestions.

Techniques for handling criticism

The first technique for dealing with criticism is to listen actively. Listening actively means trying to understand what people are telling you from their perspective. You listen actively by being involved in what the other person is saying.

When you listen actively, you ask questions and paraphrase the speaker's words to ensure you understand this person's point of view.

In emotionally charged situations, it's important to pay attention to body language that can reveal underlying emotions as well.

Even well-presented and well-intentioned criticism can feel like a personal attack. For active listening to succeed, you have to avoid being defensive. Don't judge the speaker's words until you've got a better idea of what that person is really trying to say. Really focus on what the speaker is saying. This can be especially difficult in conflict situations, where you often find yourself thinking about what you're going to say next. Try to avoid being distracted.

In a meeting with her boss, Paolo, Carla receives negative feedback about her handling of incoming calls. As she listens to Paolo go into detail about her handling of calls, she begins to get defensive. She lets some of that show in her attitude, although she hardly says a word for the entire hour they are in the conference room. The meeting does not end well. And afterwards, Carla just doesn't understand why her boss is making such a fuss about a couple of minor incidents.

Carla and Paolo's meeting might have ended quite differently if she had listened actively instead of passively. Follow along to learn how the conversation might have played out.

Paolo: Carla, there have been a couple of incidents I need to talk to you about regarding incoming phone calls.

Carla: Sure. What's wrong?

Paolo: Well, a couple of suppliers have mentioned to me that they have been kept on hold for unusually long periods while they waited for me to become available.

Carla: Did they mention why they were holding?

Paolo: Yes, because I was on another call. But I really need you to let me know when suppliers are on the other line so I can get to them quickly.

Carla: So let me just make sure I understand. You want me to interrupt your calls to let you know there's a supplier on the line, regardless of who you're currently talking to?

Paolo: Yes, with the exception of board members and the CEO. Other than that, feel free to interrupt.

Carla: OK. I definitely wasn't aware that you felt that strongly about supplier calls and I'll do that in the future.

Paolo: That would be great.

Carla: Thanks for explaining that and letting me know.

Carla displayed strong active listening skills in the previous conversation.

She asked questions that clarified Paolo's issue about supplier calls. She also paraphrased what he wanted, and, as a result, was able to understand the situation from Paolo's point of view.

In this meeting, the discussion was more collaborative and less emotionally charged.

Active listening is a key part of dealing constructively with criticism. Once you fully understand why you're being criticized, you're more likely to accept it and learn from it. But you're also in a better position to challenge the criticism if you think it's unfair. There are no set rules for this, but you can follow some guidelines to help you assess whether to challenge a criticism.

You will need to use your judgment in each situation to decide whether to challenge.

In general, when the speaker has more experience and knowledge than you do, you should probably avoid challenging the criticism.

So in part, the decision whether to challenge or not depends on the relationship and status of the person offering the critique. For example, you would apply different standards to judging whether to challenge criticism from your boss and criticism from a peer.

See each person to learn more about when to challenge.

Your boss

Although challenging someone in a senior position should often be avoided, you might consider challenging a criticism from your boss when your boss lacks key information.

For example, you may be responsible for preparing the minutes of the weekly management meeting. When your boss criticizes you for not getting the minutes out the same day, you determine that it's appropriate to challenge the criticism because your boss is unaware that the CEO must sign off on the minutes before distribution.

A peer

You may be more likely to challenge a peer who offers criticism, especially if that person lacks experience or expertise.

For instance, if another administrative professional criticizes the way you document a meeting, you might challenge that person if the admin professional is new to the company or unfamiliar with executive-level procedures.

Other factors may affect your decision to challenge. For example, you may decide to avoid challenging someone's criticism if it will make your boss look bad.

Regardless of the circumstances, if you do decide to challenge, you should do it courteously and assertively rather than aggressively.

For example, instead of telling someone she is not as experienced as you are, point out what you have learned from your experience that makes your challenge reasonable and valid.

Later in Carla and Paolo's relationship, another incident arises, but this time Carla feels it's totally unjustified, so she challenges Paolo on it. When Paolo suggests that her family responsibilities are interfering with her work, Carla tells Paolo he's being discriminatory because she's a working mother. She feels strongly that she has managed to keep interruptions to a minimum. Paolo and Carla have an acrimonious and unproductive meeting, and their relationship at work is affected for several weeks.

Although in the preceding example Carla was correct to challenge Paolo's criticism, she became defensive.

Then she was too aggressive in her challenge, describing her boss as discriminating against her.

Their relationship suffered as a result. Carla should have asserted herself without attacking her boss in return.

The third technique for handling criticism is to ask for suggestions for developing a solution. If it looks as if you will have to make a change because of the critique, ask the person making the criticism to help you develop a solution. Asking people for suggestions shows you appreciate what they have to say and you want to know how they would handle things.

For example, Kenji, an administrative professional working with the human resources manager at a computer software firm, set up a series of one-hour seminars for employees. The first seminar was well attended and seemed well received.

But one of the customer service representatives who attended sent Kenji an e-mail saying he didn't like the speaker running the seminars, and that Kenji should have been more careful in his choice.

After finding out the reasons why the representative didn't like the speaker, Kenji thanked him for candor and asked if he had any suggestions for the future. The customer service representative sent a list of recommended speakers that Kenji promised to consider for the next series.

Criticism is hard to receive. But giving constructive criticism can also be difficult, requiring thought and care in how it's presented. So it's a good idea to remember to thank the person and avoid complaining about any extra effort his suggestion may require – whether or not you believe the criticism is valid. This shows you're open to learning from others and you appreciate being provided with frank and honest feedback. This is the final step after you've listened, accepted or challenged the criticism, and asked for suggestions.

As an administrative support professional, you're bound to receive criticism from time to time. Knowing how to handle it in a positive and productive way is an important career skill.

Three techniques can help you take criticism in a way that enhances your relationships. First, you must listen actively to fully understand the other person's position. Then you must consider whether or not the criticism needs to be challenged. If it should be, you must challenge it in an appropriate way relative to the other person's status and relationship to you.

If you decide the criticism shouldn't be challenged, you will no doubt have to make some sort of correction to your behavior. Using the third technique, asking for suggestions, you can clarify what needs to be done. You should at this point remember to thank the person for speaking up about the issue.

CHAPTER V - PUTTING YOUR BEST FOOT FORWARD

CHAPTER V - Putting Your Best Foot Forward

Several best practices can help you build and maintain a positive image and make a good impression:

- projecting a positive, professional image by building credibility and maintaining authenticity,
- creating a positive work environment by communicating honestly, respecting others, and maintaining a positive attitude, and
- practicing positive office politics.

Implementing the best practices explored in this chapter will help you to put your best foot forward as an administrative professional.

BUILD CREDIBILITY AND MAINTAIN AUTHENTICITY

Build credibility and maintain authenticity

Managing your image

Do you ever wonder what your colleagues think of you? Maybe you think it's not important, but it is. The impression your colleagues have of you could have a lasting effect on your success.

As you interact with those colleagues, they're making judgments about your professionalism and abilities. And if you aren't managing the image you project, they may get the wrong impression.

You can and should take an active part in helping others form an impression of you – this is known as impression management.

Practicing impression management will help you project a positive and professional image, and, in turn, you will be trusted, respected, and admired by colleagues.

The two key tasks involved with impression management are building credibility and maintaining authenticity.

Building credibility

Credibility is all about trust and is key to a positive image. You can work on building your credibility by honoring confidentiality, keeping your promises, and accepting responsibility.

As an administrative professional, you'll be trusted with confidential information. You need to make sure this information remains confidential.

For example, you can lock it up, make sure photocopies aren't left unattended at the copy machine, discard unwanted printouts and data storage devices properly, password protect electronic information, and discuss confidential information only with those privy to it.

Another way to build credibility is to keep your promises. Failing to keep promises at work makes you look incompetent, unreliable, and unprofessional.

If you want to be trusted, you need to consistently keep your promises. And don't make promises you can't keep.

To help keep the promises you make, you should set time limits, determine the details of the promise, and confirm in writing what needs to be done.

See each task for an example of how it's used.

Set time limits

Setting time limits is essential. For example, if you're asked to perform a task, confirm whether it's a one-time promise or an ongoing commitment. Then, you should also talk to all parties involved and make sure everyone agrees on the deadline.

Determine details

Determining the details of the promise is important to delivering what's expected. You should ask questions to determine exactly what it is you need to deliver. You want to avoid failing to deliver on your promise because of a misunderstanding.

Confirm in writing

Confirming the promise in writing clarifies the promise for everyone. For example, you could send an e-mail describing the promise made. You should include information on the limits and details of the promise, as well as the agreed-upon deadline. This gives you one more chance for clarification. It also provides a documented understanding of expectations should questions arise later.

It's always best to promise less and deliver more – in other words, be conservative and realistic when you make a promise. Consider how long it will take to fulfill your obligation, and add time to overcome any unforeseen or probable delays so they don't negatively impact your ability to keep your promises.

For example, Amir has been asked to draw up plans for a new construction project. He knows that there's a good chance his coworker won't be able to deliver work he'll need to complete his job.

With this in mind, Amir adds a bit of time to his promise to deliver. This way, if he's right, he can still keep his promise, and if he's wrong, he can deliver on this promise early.

How you handle responsibility will also contribute to your credibility. Accepting responsibility involves acknowledging the work of others, acknowledging your part in failures, and not blaming others.

See each aspect of accepting responsibility to learn more about how it will help build your credibility.

Acknowledging the work of others

By acknowledging the work of others, you show that you appreciate and recognize their contributions. Be specific when describing contributions; give credit where credit is due. But, as you do this, don't negate your own contribution.

For example, if Jill, a coworker, helped with a company newsletter by supplying the photographs, give her credit. But don't give the impression that her contribution outweighs yours or anyone else's.

Acknowledging your part in failures

When your contributions fail to produce acceptable or desired results, you must also be ready to acknowledge your part in the failure. It's best to state what went wrong, and then move forward with suggestions to address the failure.

For example, perhaps a package you sent failed to be delivered on time. After following up with the courier, you find that in your haste to send the package, you transposed the numbers in the address. You create and save a verified shipping label for future use, to avoid this happening again.

Not blaming others

When you do fail, don't blame others – acknowledge your part in the failure. Placing blame for your actions on others is irresponsible.

For example, if you were unable to complete your work because your coworker was late getting information to you. Accept responsibility, don't draw attention to the fact your coworker let you down.

Question

Which actions can you take to build your credibility?

Options:

1. Honor confidentiality
2. Keep promises
3. Accept responsibility
4. Build alliances
5. Avoid confrontation

Answer:

Option 1: This option is correct. Always honoring confidentiality demonstrates your trustworthiness, and therefore builds credibility.

Option 2: This option is correct. Before making a promise, make sure you can keep it. Failure to keep a promise will damage your credibility.

Option 3: This option is correct. Accepting responsibility involves acknowledging both the work of others and your part in failures, and not placing blame.

Option 4: This option is incorrect. Building alliances with colleagues isn't part of building credibility. However, this may happen as part of office politics.

Option 5: This option is incorrect. Avoiding confrontation isn't a way to build credibility and will probably damage it.

Maintaining authenticity

Projecting a positive professional image also requires that you maintain your authenticity. Feeling good about yourself, being your true self, and building your personal brand will help you be authentic.

Being authentic happens over time and is a reflection of the choices you make. When you consistently act in a way that's true to who you are, it helps to build trust, as your colleagues come to know what to expect from you.

You should be proactive in your efforts to feel good about yourself. This entails rebutting your inner critic, looking after yourself, and getting help from others when you need it.

Rebut your inner critic by silencing the negative self-talk that sometimes goes on in your head. Try instead to generate positive thoughts. You will accomplish more with a positive attitude.

Question

For example, Neil is thinking about an upcoming task. His thoughts center on how he struggled with a similar task previously. He concentrates on what he did wrong in an attempt to avoid the same mistakes again.

Is this the best way for Neil to be thinking?

Options:

1. Yes
2. No

Answer:

Option 1: This is incorrect. Neil is only feeding his negativity. He should focus on what he did right or what he learned the first time.

Option 2: This is correct. It would be better if Neil focused on the fact that he has already done the task once and how his experience will help him do a better job this time.

Looking after yourself helps to build your confidence and self-worth.

Kendra admires Rena, one of her coworkers. Rena is always happy, gets her work done, and is confident. Kendra asks Rena how she does it. Rena tells her that she does have to work at it, but some healthy habits help.

See each habit to find out what Rena told Kendra.

Stay fit

"I take the time to stay fit. I try to eat right, sleep right, and exercise. It helps me feel better both physically and mentally and in turn I'm more positive about myself."

Have fun

"I make time for fun. You can't work all the time! I try to balance my work and personal life. For instance, I have lunch every Friday with some of my girlfriends."

Remember accomplishments

"I've created a scrapbook of the things I'm most proud of in both my personal and professional life. When I'm feeling down, I take a look at it and it helps me remember my accomplishments, which usually turns my mood around."

Another way to feel good about yourself is to get help from others. Spend time with positive, supportive people – their positive energy and attitudes can do wonders for your own attitude.

For instance, attend a social gathering, a sporting event, or just hang out with family or friends. You may read something inspirational or watch a funny or empowering movie. Do whatever helps you maintain or regain your positive attitude.

Another component of maintaining your authenticity is to be your true self. You can't maintain a false image, and if you try, it'll ultimately damage your image. People won't know what to expect from you, and in turn won't trust you either.

Flaunting your uniqueness is a technique you can use to accentuate your individuality. For example, Sean loves trivia. Everywhere he goes he has trivia cards and he pulls them out from time to time to break tension, lighten a mood, or just build a relationship.

"True to yourself" decision making is guided by what's important to you and reflects your authentic self. For example, Hilda often feels uncomfortable saying "No" when asked to take on tasks at work – even when she doesn't have time, or when the tasks are unsuitable for her skill level. When Hilda learns to respect her authentic self and to say "No," she finds her work more enjoyable, and, to her surprise, is offered tasks that are more in line with her interests and abilities.

Often, the traits most valued by others are trustworthiness, caring, humility, and capability. Working to project these traits would be a good place to start with your own personal brand.

But, to be effective, the traits you choose to project need to align with your true or authentic self. Building your personal brand requires you to do certain things: know what's important to you, be consistent, and build on your uniqueness, values, and strengths.

Question

What can you do to maintain your authenticity?

Options:

1. Feel good about yourself
2. Be your true self

3. Build your personal brand

4. Avoid overly positive people

5. Be careful to guard your true character

Answer:

Option 1: This option is correct. Feeling good about yourself will help build your confidence and self- worth, helping you to maintain your authenticity.

Option 2: This option is correct. Trying to project an image that doesn't match your true self will damage the way others view you. Authenticity can only be achieved when you're true to yourself.

Option 3: This option is correct. Building a personal brand can help you maintain your authenticity because it helps you consistently project traits that are important to you.

Option 4: This option is incorrect. Spending time with people who have positive energy will make you feel good about yourself, which in turn will help you maintain your authenticity.

Option 5: This option is incorrect. In order to maintain authenticity, you need to be your true self.

Case Study: Question 1 of 2

Scenario

For your convenience, the case study is repeated with each question.

Jax works for a medical clinic and has a reputation as a joker. One of the doctors asks him to provide a report on the incidence of patients presenting with flu-like symptoms by Friday afternoon. The doctor gives him some of the patient records he will need for the report. Jax is a bit apprehensive about the task.

Help Jax build credibility and maintain authenticity by answering the questions.

Question

Which are examples of things Jax could do to build credibility?

Options:

1. As Jax leaves his desk, he locks all the patient files in his desk drawer and locks his workstation

2. Jax asks the doctor how far back he wants him to go, the level of detail expected about each case, and confirms a 2:00 p.m. deadline for Friday

3. Jax credits Andrea for her help with identifying all the relevant cases, relaying how it helped him compile and generate the report

4. Jax asks Andrea to help him and delegates the majority of the work to her because he's too busy to do it himself

5. Jax immediately agrees to have the report ready by Friday afternoon

Answer:

Option 1: This option is correct. By protecting confidential information, Jax is honoring confidentiality. Option 2: This option is correct. Confirming details of the promise he's making will help Jax keep his commitment and build credibility.

Option 3: This option is correct. It's important to acknowledge the work of others. It helps to build credibility by showing others that you recognize and appreciate their efforts.

Option 4: This option is incorrect. If you can't keep a promise, don't make it. Passing work you promised to do on to someone else is not a credible action.

Option 5: This option is incorrect. While the doctor may be impressed with Jax's eagerness, because Jax didn't confirm what's expected, he may inadvertently fail to deliver on his promise.

Case Study: Question 2 of 2

Which examples demonstrate what Jax could do to maintain authenticity?

Options:

1. When Jax returns to his desk, he realizes he's having negative thoughts, but recalling past successes helps him think positive thoughts

2. Jax is known for being a bit of a clown, and, true to form, jokes about the doctor's request being unusual

3. Jax decides to try a different approach with the doctor and acts more serious than usual

4. Jax agrees to complete the report even though he doesn't believe he can do it on time

Answer:

Option 1: This option is correct. Negative self-talk won't get you where you want to go. As soon as you recognize the negativity, try your best to turn your thoughts to the positive.

Option 2: This option is correct. Because Jax has a reputation for being a joker and he and the doctor have an established relationship, Jax can get away with this kind of informality. He's just flaunting his uniqueness.

Option 3: This option is incorrect. Jax needs to stay true to his character if he's going to maintain his authenticity.

Option 4: This option is incorrect. Jax should never make a promise he can't keep. If he fails to deliver on this promise, it will damage his image with the doctor and anybody else relying on the report.

Because your professional image is so important to your success, you need to take action to manage the impression you make. Building credibility and maintaining authenticity are two ways you can project a positive, professional image.

Build your credibility by honoring confidentiality, keeping your promises, and accepting responsibility.

Being authentic means you're consistently true to the person you are. You can maintain your authenticity by making an effort to feel good about yourself, be your true self, and build your personal brand.

COUNTERACT A NEGATIVE WORK ENVIRONMENT

Counteract a negative work environment

Creating a positive work environment

Administrative professionals play a vital role in establishing a positive work environment, which is key to any organization's long-term success. But what if a negative environment pervades an organization? It can be difficult to be positive in this case, and you could find yourself contributing to the negative atmosphere.

For example, Kristine, an administrative support professional, works in a Marketing Department that has low morale and productivity. Follow along as Kristine interacts with her colleagues.

Due to the Marketing Department's high turnover rate, Kristine is constantly recruiting. She always arrives on time for meetings with HR, but she often has to wait for others to arrive. While waiting she often gossips with a colleague in the HR office. In a recent HR meeting, she expresses her displeasure with the constant recruiting and says she fears it will never end.

A colleague has approached Kristine to request a meeting with the VP of Marketing. Kristine reluctantly stops what she is doing to schedule the appointment. She is very busy and makes it known that she is not thrilled with this interruption.

During a meeting, one of Kristine's colleagues asks for her help. Kristine expresses surprise that he needs help with such an easy task. However, she eventually agrees to help.

Kristine is contributing to a negative work environment by gossiping, being rude, and showing a lack of respect and support for her colleagues. But you can avoid being a negative influence, counteract a negative environment, and help create a positive one by communicating honestly, respecting others, and maintaining a positive attitude.

Communicate honestly

Communicating honestly requires that you watch how you say things, be attentive, and don't gossip. Remember, it's not always what you say, but how you say it.

See each example of Macie saying the same sentence and notice how its meaning changes based on how she says it.

Macie disrespectful

"What are you doing?" In this instance, Macie sounds like she's surprised, but not in a good way. Her tone suggests she is questioning what you are doing and comes across as disrespectful.

Macie smiling

"What are you doing?" Voiced this way, Macie sounds curious and intrigued. Her interest shows support in what you are doing.

Macie judgmental

"What are you doing?" This time Macie sounds alarmed and her tone conveys judgment. Spoken to this way, you will probably feel as though she doesn't trust you.

Only 7% of our communication style is made up of the actual words we say. The other 93% is how you say those words.

So, carefully choose how you express yourself, including the tone of your voice and the pace of your speech. The result will be increasingly honest and effective communication.

Now consider this situation. Jazmine needs to speak to the VP of Finance. After waiting patiently to be acknowledged by the VP's administrative support professional Claire, Jazmine interrupts Claire's personal call.

Claire ends the call but fails to make eye contact or engage in the conversation any more than necessary. Even worse, Claire acts as though Jazmine is being a nuisance. Then, when Jazmine is explaining her reasons for wanting to see the VP, Claire interrupts to say that the VP is too busy today. Jazmine is frustrated, and decides that in future she'll insist on speaking directly to the VP of Finance.

The previous example demonstrates a failure to be attentive. Being attentive helps you communicate honestly. You can express interest and attentiveness by taking a few actions:

- make eye contact and smile,
- ask for opinions and compliment work,
- use names and acknowledge the person, and
- ask for and receive suggestions respectfully.

Question

Keeping the actions for showing attentiveness in mind, what are some things Claire could have done differently when speaking to Jazmine?

Options:

1. End her personal call immediately and address Jazmine
2. Smile and use Jazmine's name as she helps her
3. Make eye contact and ask Jazmine how she can help her
4. Acknowledge Jazmine and tell her she'd be right with her
5. Finish her phone call and wait for Jazmine to approach her
6. Let Jazmine finish explaining her reasons for wanting to see the VP

Answer:

Option 1: This option is correct. Part of being attentive is acknowledging those you're interacting with.

Option 2: This option is correct. Smiling and using the person's name conveys interest.

Option 3: This option is correct. Making eye contact and speaking directly to the person helps establish a good working rapport.

Option 4: This option is incorrect. A personal call should never take precedence over a business matter. Claire should have ended the personal call immediately and focused her attention on Jazmine.

Option 5: This option is incorrect. Claire should have ended the call immediately and offered her attention and assistance to Jazmine.

Option 6: This is a correct option. Claire should listen to what Jazmine has to say – an important way of showing attentiveness.

In addition to watching how you say things and being attentive, you should avoid gossiping. In short, don't repeat or share anything you wouldn't say directly to a person. Also avoid listening to gossip – you don't want to be guilty by association, or risk a loss of respect and trust.

Participating in gossip is a sure way to lose the respect and trust of your colleagues. They may begin to wonder what you say about them.

In general, you should keep conversations focused on work-related issues, or neutral topics.

Liam, an administrative support professional, uses honest communication to help counteract a negative environment. He has been asked to help Georgina write a proposal. Georgina has a reputation for being difficult to work with.

Follow along as Liam discusses Georgina's proposal with her.

Liam: Well, there are a few issues, but nothing that can't be fixed easily. Georgina: Great, but before we get into that, did you know anything about the scandal surrounding the Henderson project?

Liam: No. But I'd like to focus on your proposal, if you don't mind.

Georgina: Fair enough. I don't know who wrote the guidelines for this, but they sure didn't know what they were doing. I can't figure out when to use which template.

Liam: I understand, and I think I can help. What do you need to know? Georgina: Can you explain why we have so many different templates and when I should use each one?

Liam: Absolutely! Actually, I have a really great job aid for template selection saved on my computer. I'll send it to you. Once you review it, if you have any questions, just let me know.

Liam applies the techniques of honest communication during his conversation with Georgina to help counteract her negativity:

- First, Liam avoided gossiping by tactfully steering the conversation back to the proposal. This helped focus Georgina's efforts.
- Then, Liam listened attentively as Georgina explained herself. This helped Georgina feel comfortable.
- In addition, Liam was careful to make sure his tone was positive and encouraging, especially when giving constructive criticism.

When you're consistently honest in the way you communicate, others will notice and may strive to do the same when working with you.

A benefit of the positive environment created by communicating honestly is that coworkers will contribute more ideas because they feel valued and listened to.

Question

Hugh is an administrative support professional. His company is working on a project and unanticipated pitfalls have lowered team morale. As everyone watches the clock, the meeting to decide on a path forward is quickly becoming unproductive. Hugh is even hearing about Jim's supposed affair.

Which actions can Hugh take to support a positive work environment through honest communication?

Options:

1. Pay attention to the tone in your voice as you correct a misunderstanding about an important project objective

2. Ask the team members to take turns speaking and listen carefully to what each has to say

3. Avoid and discourage any nonwork related discussions, especially gossip

4. Focus attention by sternly demanding the team "focus on the task at hand"

5. Interrupt a colleague's contributions to question her "faulty" logic

Answer:

Option 1: This option is correct. When communicating honestly, you need to be more careful about how you say things than what you say. Said with the wrong tone, most anything can be offensive and therefore counterproductive.

Option 2: This option is correct. Being attentive is a great way to encourage a positive work environment. Just like you, when your colleagues are listened to, it makes them feel valued and appreciated. This can help improve morale and productivity.

Option 3: This option is correct. Gossip, personal or professional in nature, should be avoided at all times. Participating in gossip will cause you to lose the respect and trust of your colleagues.

Option 4: This option is incorrect. Being stern with a group of colleagues is likely to incite more negativity. Always maintain a positive, professional tone while engaged in conversations at work.

Option 5: This option is incorrect. You shouldn't interrupt to correct someone's argument – you're not being attentive. Everyone deserves to be heard and respected for the contributions they make.

Respect others

Another way to create a positive work environment is to respect others. Some say respect needs to be earned, and that may be true. However, in professional situations, you'll find that showing respect is a good way to earn it.

Respecting others helps to build a positive environment.

And two important benefits of respecting others are improved productivity and self-esteem. When respect for others is encouraged and upheld, people tend to contribute more ideas. This can be helpful for solving problems or innovating.

You can help promote these benefits by treating others with respect – be honest, be dependable, and be punctual.

Honest communication is productive, constructive, and positive. When you're being honest, all communication is done with the intention of being helpful and practical.

For instance, even though you might be thinking your colleague made a mistake, your response should be positive and constructive. Mention any good points first, and then carefully explain the mistake and provide ways to improve in future. Avoid placing blame.

Being dependable and punctual are also important:

- Being dependable means your colleagues can count on you. Taking initiative, meeting deadlines, and completing tasks thoroughly can help you establish your dependability.

- Being punctual is important because it demonstrates that you value your colleagues' time, you're ready to contribute, and you recognize the importance of the task at hand.

Recall Liam and Georgina. They're meeting again about the proposal. Liam was busy at his desk, but set an alarm to remind him of his meeting. He knows that being punctual will demonstrate the respect Georgina deserves. Follow along as Liam continues to use respect to help create a positive work environment.

Liam: The proposal is very well laid out. But I did notice a couple of things about the summary. It's just a bit unclear because you seem to introduce new information in the second and third paragraphs. I suggest you consider whether this information should be in the proposal itself. If not, you should remove any reference to the material not covered.

Georgina: Thanks, Liam. I can see that you did a thorough job on the review, and your input is very helpful.

Liam demonstrated respect for Georgina by showing up on time for their meeting. His thorough review of her proposal demonstrated his dependability, and he gave honest, helpful feedback.

Question

Lorraine works as an administrative support professional for a talent agency. She promised to call a hopeful client, Diane, at 3:00 p.m. and now she's calling her at 3:45 p.m. Lorraine knows Diane is hoping to land a TV commercial that's currently looking for actors. She hasn't reviewed Diane's portfolio, although she was supposed to in order to validate her boss's opinion that Diane is best suited to voiceover work.

Diane wants to talk to Lorraine's boss, who's out of the office until Monday. Without even reviewing her portfolio, Lorraine tells Diane that this wasn't the right opportunity for her.

How could Lorraine have built a positive working environment by showing respect for Diane?

Options:

1. She could have kept her promise to call Diane at 3:00 p.m.

2. She could have told Diane the truth

3. She could have reviewed Diane's portfolio like she was expected to

4. She could have put off telling Diane and waited to talk to her boss on Monday

5. She could have told Diane that her face is just not right for commercials

Answer:

Option 1: This is correct. Being punctual is an important part of respecting others. Punctuality shows respect for other peoples' time.

Option 2: This is correct. Honesty is key to respecting others. If handled with care and respect, people can learn from the truth, no matter how disappointing it might be.

Option 3: This is correct. Doing a job consistently and properly helps build dependability, which in turn helps to create a positive work environment.

Option 4: This is incorrect. Putting off the inevitable won't help Diane. It's better to be direct and professional.

Option 5: This is incorrect. You should be truthful but respectful when being honest. Be helpful; not hurtful. You should phrase your comments carefully.

Maintain a positive attitude

Attitude is contagious. And a positive attitude is more helpful and productive than a negative one. As an administrative support professional, it's part of your job to help your organization be as productive as possible. And maintaining a positive attitude can help you do this.

One benefit of maintaining a positive attitude is that it helps motivate employees to come to work. Wouldn't you rather spend your day working in a positive environment instead of a negative one?

Being optimistic and enthusiastic is a good way to maintain a positive attitude. It also sets the tone for everyone you come in contact with.

Luca, an administrative professional, is helping with a chemical engineering project to improve an industrial cleanser. So far, many formulations have failed to produce any significant change in the effectiveness of the cleanser. Luca remains positive and cheers the team on by saying that each failure is a step closer to success. The team has been impressed with Luca's continued optimism and enthusiasm.

Maintaining a sense of humor can also encourage a positive work environment.

Laughter releases stress, builds relationships, changes attitudes, and energizes people. But be mindful of your use of humor – never use it to make fun of others. And never use politically incorrect humor.

Georgina has just told Liam that she has submitted her proposal. She's stressed and worried about it. Follow along as Liam tries to cheer her up.

Liam: Georgina, you worked really hard on that proposal. You did an excellent job! It's clear and persuasive and will be accepted.

Georgina: Thanks Liam. I suppose you're right. I shouldn't worry.

Liam: That's right! Besides you can always blame me if the proposal sinks.

Georgina was still a bit negative about the proposal, but Liam was able to improve her attitude by being enthusiastic about her work. And he used humor to lighten the mood.

Question

You have learned that you can create a positive work environment by communicating honestly, respecting others, and being positive.

Which are benefits of creating a positive work environment?

Options:

1. Employees are more likely to contribute ideas
2. Employees are more productive and have higher self-esteem
3. Employees are more committed to their jobs
4. Employees are more motivated to come to work
5. Employees are more knowledgeable about their jobs
6. Employees are more likely to take shorter vacations

Answer:

Option 1: This option is correct. One reason employees may contribute more is that they know they'll be treated with respect.

Option 2: This option is correct. Treating others with respect has a positive impact on their productivity and self-esteem.

Option 3: This option is correct. When employees are treated honestly, they're more likely to be committed to the job because they see the company is committed to them.

Option 4: This option is correct. When the work atmosphere is positive and efforts are made to maintain a positive attitude, employees are more motivated to come to work each day.

Option 5: This option is incorrect. A positive work environment will not directly impact employees' job knowledge.

Option 6: This option is incorrect. Even though they enjoy coming to work, employees are likely to still take the vacation time allotted them.

Case Study: Question 1 of 2

Scenario

Min-Jee works as an administrative support professional for a consulting firm. She has been asked to attend a team meeting for a project she knows is behind schedule and over budget. She has also noticed that the team members involved with the project are very stressed.

Answer the questions, in the order given, to help the team take action to counteract the negative environment.

Question

Min-Jee is nervous because she's not all that clear why she's being asked to join the meeting. She grabs the information she was asked to bring, even though time constraints kept her from doing a thorough job compiling it. As she waits for the meeting to begin, she asks Jordan if he's heard anything about pending layoffs, and whether Mary in Marketing has been let go. She has heard rumors and wants to know what he's heard.

Which actions will counteract the negative atmosphere in this situation?

Options:

1. Jordan expresses his unwillingness to discuss the topic of layoffs and changes the subject to the matter at hand

2. Min-Jee decides that from now on she will check her time constraints and make realistic commitments 3. Min-Jee shakes off her nervousness and assumes that her input is sought because she can help

4. Jordan promises to tell Min-Jee what he's heard so long as she promises not to repeat it

5. Min-Jee decides to hold back information until she sees why she was asked to participate

Answer:

Option 1: This option is correct. Jordan is right to avoid getting involved in office gossip. Gossip damages reputations and destroys trust.

Option 2: This option is correct. Min-Jee must be dependable if she hopes to contribute to a positive work environment. She can start by doing all tasks well.

Option 3: This option is correct. Being optimistic about her involvement will help Min-Jee be a positive influence on the project.

Option 4: This option is incorrect. Participating in gossip is unacceptable under all circumstances. If you wouldn't say it to a person's face, don't say it at all.

Option 5: This option is incorrect. All communication should be honest. This means providing all the helpful and relevant information you have.

Case Study: Question 2 of 2

One of the team members starts to talk about how this is all the project manager's fault. The discussion about the project manager continues for quite some time.

The team lead then asks Min-Jee for her opinion on one of her colleagues' ideas. "That won't work" is her hasty and dismissive reply.

Which actions will help counteract the negativity in this situation?

Options:

1. Min-Jee rephrases her reply, being careful of the tone she uses

2. Min-Jee reminds the team that it's unproductive to place blame and suggests they focus on the issue 3. Jordan jokes "Sure blame the project manager, I bet no one's ever done that before"

4. Min-Jee disagrees with blaming the project manager and insists everyone share the blame

5. Jordan agrees with Jin-Mee's comment that the idea will never work

Answer:

Option 1: This option is correct. You need to be careful about how you say what you say, otherwise you may send the wrong message.

Option 2: This option is correct. Min-Jee is right to switch the focus back to the issue at hand. Honest communication is practical and helpful. It's not very constructive to spend time blaming someone.

Option 3: This option is correct. Jordan's use of humor is likely to lighten the mood by relieving some stress. Generally, humor is appropriate so long as it isn't personal or political.

Option 4: This option is incorrect. Placing blame is never productive and should be avoided. Instead focus on resolving the problem itself.

Option 5: This option is incorrect. If Jordan has a comment to add, he should keep it optimistic. Adding to the negativity won't move the team toward a solution.

Helping to create a positive work environment is one of the most effective things you can do. As an administrative professional, you're in touch with your colleagues on a daily basis. And attitude is infectious, so if yours is positive, you'll have a positive impact.

Strive to be honest in your communication, respect others, and maintain a positive attitude in all your workplace interactions. Your efforts will contribute to a more productive work environment and provide great benefit to your organization.

PRACTICING POSITIVE OFFICE POLITICS

Practicing positive office politics

Practicing positive office politics

For most administrative professionals, "office politics" is something other people practice. And they often

view those who engage in it as manipulators who scheme, spread rumors, and kiss up, while hard- working colleagues are busy implementing strategies, opening up communication, and building relationships.

But the truth about office politics is that everybody participates. "Playing politics" is a natural outcome when people with different interests, experiences, and agendas work together.

Office politics can be defined simply as informal actions that influence decision making about who gets what, when, where, and how. Basically, it's the skill of managing people and perception.

Office politics aren't something to be afraid of. In fact, office politics are an essential part of organizational success.

It may help if you think about it not as playing politics, but as understanding organizational dynamics – the network of communication and relationships in your workplace.

By avoiding the negative aspects and leveraging the positive aspects of office politics, administrative support professionals can promote strong values and broaden their spheres of influence.

There are three key guidelines for practicing positive office politics:

- know your boss's objectives, and contribute to achieving them,
- collaborate, rather than compete, and
- respect the chain of command.

Support and contribute

As an administrative support professional, your relationship with your boss should be mutually enriching, with each of you pursuing goals that benefit both the organization and your careers.

This means it's very important to know your boss's objectives, and contribute to achieving them. Sometimes, a day at work can seem like an endless series of conflicts. But let's face it. It's impractical
and counterproductive to fight every battle with equal intensity.

So, the first tactic for achieving your boss's objectives is to choose your battles wisely – decide what's really worth expending your energy on.

Every day you make choices that affect other people. And if you're not selective, you're not effective. You need to focus on issues that support your boss's objectives and your organization's values.

If you find yourself wanting to respond rigidly to a situation, ask yourself "How much does this really matter?" You may find that conceding a point will give you credit down the line.

Sometimes, the main competitor for your time and attention is yourself.

The second tactic for achieving your boss's objectives is to make sure you don't pursue individual goals that conflict with the goals of your boss or the organization.

As an administrative support professional, you have to be careful that you align personal and corporate interests.

Personal goals are not necessarily incompatible with organizational goals. Many workplaces prosper because they provide opportunities for personal growth to their staff. But when workers pursue personal goals that are contrary to corporate values and interests, it can have a negative impact.

Quinton works as an administrative support professional for a construction company that's owned by his boss, Henry. The company is growing, and budgetary concerns are always an issue. Henry is organized and professional, but isn't very adept at using a computer. Follow along as Quinton discusses his boss's objectives and how he contributes to achieving them.

Quinton: I only have so much time and energy, so I know it's important to choose my battles wisely. For example, Henry and I usually come to an agreement about costing issues. But sometimes he'll decide to work with vendor A, when I'd prefer vendor B. I may not agree, but I need to move on and try to make his decision work. Otherwise, nothing will get done. *Quinton says*

Quinton: I decide which computer software to purchase and install for my boss and myself. I have to consider cost, compatibility, and ease of use. There are some programs that I prefer, but I know that the interface would be difficult for my boss to handle. They'd also put a strain on the budget.

So, as long as they do the job, I choose simpler, less pricey software packages, even if they aren't my personal favorites. *Quinton says*

Question

Alden is an administrative support professional working for a commercial real estate company. He hopes to open his own office some day.

Which examples reflect positive tactics Alden uses for contributing to his boss's objectives?

Options:

1. Although he had to make a special trip, Alden uses a local supplier for office supplies because it has ties to the community that could prove useful to his company

2. When a dispute over the booking of meeting rooms erupts, Alden politely defers to the other party and finds an alternate room for his boss to use

3. Alden uses the company database to compile a list of potential clients for the day he opens his own office

4. Alden leaves work early to attend classes to get his real estate license

Answer:

Option 1: This option is correct. In this example, Alden makes sure not to pursue individual goals that conflict with the goals of the organization. Although it's inconvenient for him, Alden uses the local office supplies company because the relationship is an investment for his company.

Option 2: This option is correct. In this example, Alden is choosing his battles wisely. In the long run, the issue won't make any difference, and now he may have some credit he can use for a decision that really matters.

Option 3: This option is incorrect. Alden shouldn't pursue individual goals that conflict with the goals of his boss.

Option 4: This option is incorrect. Alden's personal professional development is important to him, but it isn't an example of contributing to his boss's objectives.

Collaborate with others

As an administrative support professional, you know that your decisions and actions have a major effect on your working relationship with your boss. But, when you join an organization, you become part of a social infrastructure – connected to everyone else that works there. These connections mean that your decisions and actions also affect the work of your colleagues.

A keen sense of competition can help stimulate successful business practices in the marketplace.

But when that competitive drive is turned inwards, it can disrupt and destroy your organization's social infrastructure.

To build strength from within, it's important to collaborate, rather than compete with your colleagues. Two key tactics for collaborating well are don't act superior and don't overprotect your turf.

See each tactic to learn more.

Don't act superior

Don't act superior or try to upstage your colleagues when you challenge their position. You're more likely to get your point across if you have a sense of calm and composure when you offer your point of view. Present your position as a win-win situation.

Don't overprotect your turf

Don't overprotect your turf or try to make yourself indispensable. It shows coworkers you don't trust them, and causes problems if you're not there when an issue erupts. Instead, think about building relationships and influencing people through an exchange of value – in this case, information and trust.

You can also take two positive actions when collaborating:

Do listen to others. When you treat your colleagues with respect and show you value their input, they will respond in kind.

Do share information and make sure your colleagues know what it is you're trying to achieve. When you work as a team, you can solve problems more effectively and also share the credit when things go right.

Follow along with Quinton, the administrative support professional at the construction company, as he talks about how he uses collaboration and cooperation in his position.

Quinton: When I first started working in administrative support, I thought the best way to make myself valuable was to be indispensable to the company. I channeled all decisions through myself, and I tried to control our departmental resources. Soon, I noticed my coworkers were becoming uncommunicative. At my first performance review, I found out they thought I was acting superior, and that I didn't trust their opinions. *Quinton is serious*

Quinton: Now that I've gained professional experience, I've learned that my colleagues are my most valuable resource. I practice collaboration, not competition when I deal with others. I share information with them, and make sure they're clear on what I'm trying to achieve. For example, recently, my boss was preparing a proposal for a new client. Shelley, our draftsperson, worked late to make sure our blueprints were perfect. She never would have done that for the "old me." *Quinton says*

Question

Fran is an administrative support professional working on a demographic data collection project for a marketing firm.

Which examples reflect positive tactics Fran uses for collaborating with others?

Options:

1. Fran offers to facilitate the team brainstorming sessions to make sure each person has a chance to speak up and offer ideas

2. When the project leader praises Fran's work, she credits her teammates and passes on the compliment to them

3. To increase her value to the team, Fran makes sure to proof and approve all official correspondence with clients

4. When a decision about data compilation comes up, Fran makes sure her teammates know this is her area of expertise

Answer:

Option 1: This option is correct. Fran is practicing positive office politics by listening to her teammates. This is an important part of collaborating with others.

Option 2: This option is correct. By sharing information, Fran is demonstrating openness and trust with her teammates. This encourages collaboration.

Option 3: This option is incorrect. Fran should not be making herself indispensable to the team. This could be perceived as upstaging, and have a negative effect on collaboration.

Option 4: This option is incorrect. Fran isn't going to encourage collaboration by acting superior to her teammates.

Respect the chain of command

One of the more challenging tasks you'll have as an administrative support professional is understanding and interpreting how power is distributed at your workplace. This formal line of authority, communication, and responsibility within an organization is known as the chain of command.

Would you complain to the CEO of the company if you needed a new piece of office equipment? Probably not. It's important to respect the chain of command and determine where you and your coworkers fit within it.

The last thing you need is to create hard feelings with someone in authority, or someone who could be of help to you in the future.

If you bypass a peer or a superior when you're giving information or requesting a decision, it undermines the authority and position of the person who's ignored.

The first step in respecting the chain of command is to go directly to the source – the person for whom you have a request, concern, or complaint.

In this way, you'll be able to make progress with your objectives, and stop problems before they get out of hand.

But there may be times when an issue needs to be escalated up the chain of command. Perhaps someone is ignoring your request, or isn't dealing with you in a truthful manner. Perhaps they don't want to take responsibility for a decision. In cases like these, you may have to speak to a superior. If the situation isn't resolved, continue on up the chain of command.

Quinton has moved to a new job at a national publishing company – executive administrative support professional to the president. Now, he has to deal with the chain of command in a large organization. Alisha is a junior administrative support professional who Quinton has been mentoring. Alisha is new at the job and is having issues getting her ideas heard. Follow along as the two colleagues discuss the chain of command at their workplace.

Quinton: Alisha! Where are you off to in such a hurry?

Alisha: I'm tired of people not paying attention to what I have to say. I'm going straight to the top this time. *Alisha says angrily.*

Quinton: Let's talk first. We have a chain of command you have to go through if you have an issue. What's the problem?

Alisha: My boss has a manuscript by a new author he's really keen on. But as you know he's in charge of non-fiction, and this is a novel. I've tried everything to get it to the head of fiction, but his assistant Danny keeps blocking my access. Danny is sneaky and doesn't want anyone else to get credit.

Quinton: If you've hit a roadblock, you can't go storming in to the president's office. How will the head of fiction feel if the president thinks she has missed a potential best-seller?

Alisha: I never thought of that. I'd be in her bad books for life.

Quinton: You should always go the source of your problem first. But if you're stuck, and a compromise isn't possible, then you should escalate your issue one step up the chain of command. Why don't you contact the head of fiction directly and ask if she'll read the manuscript? But don't badmouth Danny, maybe you could include an extra copy for him to read.

Alisha: I'll do that. Thanks, Quinton.

Quinton helped Alisha by reminding her about the chain of command. He told her that she should go to the source of her problem, and then escalate the issue only if it can't be resolved at that level. Quinton respected the chain of command at the publishing company.

Question

Mira is an administrative support professional at a financial services company. She handles very sensitive financial information, and is responsible for protecting the privacy of clients. Recently, Mira has discovered that Jason, a computer technician, has bypassed security protocols and accessed her computer to play games after hours.

In what order should Mira handle this situation with respect to the chain of command?

Options:

A. Mira should speak directly to Jason

B. Mira should speak with Jason's supervisor

C. Mira should speak to Jason's supervisor's boss D. Mira should go to the top of the command chain

Answer:

Mira should speak directly to Jason is ranked the first step in the chain of command. Mira's first choice should be to go to the source of the problem – and speak directly to Jason.

Mira should speak with Jason's supervisor is ranked the second step in the chain of command. If Mira can't resolve her problem with Jason, she needs to speak with his supervisor – one step up the chain of command.

Mira should speak to Jason's supervisor's boss is ranked the third step in the chain of command. If Mira still has an issue after speaking with the supervisor, she needs to try and resolve the issue with his boss.

Mira should go to the top of the command chain is ranked the fourth step in the chain of command. Mira's last step would be to go to the top of the chain of command.

Playing politics

Playing politics isn't a substitute for knowledge and hard work, but if you want to succeed, managing your political environment is just as important as managing your tasks and responsibilities.

Question

Amal is a senior administrative support professional in the Human Resources Department of a large advertising agency.

Which are examples that reflect tactics Amal can use for practicing positive office politics?

Options:

1. Amal takes the initiative to complete and submit his boss's expense reports by the deadline

2. Amal works cooperatively with his fellow support staff to work out an equitable departmental budget

3. When a junior colleague complains she hasn't been given credit on a project, Amal encourages her to

speak to the project leader directly

Essential Skills for Administrative Support Professionals

4. Amal keeps his work to himself to avoid his ideas being poached by coworkers

5. Amal makes sure all budgetary decisions for the department are channeled through him

Answer:

Option 1: This option is correct. Taking the initiative to complete a task is an example of knowing your boss's objectives and contributing to achieving them.

Option 2: This option is correct. Working cooperatively toward an equitable solution is an example of collaborating, rather than competing, with coworkers.

Option 3: This option is correct. Speaking to the project leader is an example of respecting the chain of command.

Option 4: This option is incorrect. Overprotecting your turf shows coworkers you mistrust them. It can also cause problems if a situation erupts and you're not there to fix it.

Option 5: This option is incorrect. Amal shouldn't try to be indispensable. He needs to share knowledge and communicate with his colleagues.

The three key guidelines for practicing positive office politics are to know your boss's objectives and contribute to achieving them; to collaborate, rather than compete with your colleagues; and to respect the chain of command at your workplace.

REFERENCES

References

Administrative Assistant's and Secretary's Handbook, Third Edition - 2008, James Stroman, Kevin Wilson, and Jennifer Wauson

Managing Up: 59 Ways to Build a Career-Advancing Relationship with Your Boss - 2000, Michael Dobson

Building a Partnership with Your Boss - 1999, Jerry Wisinski

Let's Talk! More No-Nonsense Advice for Project Success - 2007, Neal Whitten, Management Concepts

The Valuable Office Professional: For Administrative Assistants, Office Managers, Secretaries, and Other Support Staff - 1997, Michelle Burke

GLOSSARY

Glossary

A

administrative support professional - A person who serves as assistant to a supervisor, manager, or team leader in an organization. The duties of this position vary widely from one organization to another.

aggressive communication style - Method of expression in which one is offensive, does not consider the position or thoughts of others, and attacks people as well as issues. These communicators are ruled by emotions rather than reason, and they often lose control.

assertive communication style - Method of expression in which people communicate their own ideas and feelings, while respecting other people's feelings. These communicators speak respectfully about results or problems beyond their control. They're self-respecting, self-expressive, and straightforward.

C

chain of command - The hierarchy of individuals within an organization.

communication skills - The ability to send and receive information effectively.

I

interpersonal dynamics - The interactions and motivating forces that influence patterns of personal interaction and communication within a group.

interpersonal skills - The ability to effectively manage situations and achieve objectives through social communication and interaction.

O

office politics - The manipulation or control of interpersonal dynamics to achieve a desired result within the workplace.

organizational and management skills - The ability to plan, schedule, and understand how one's job fits within the scope of an organization.

P

passive communication style - Method of expression in which people don't engage with other people; they withdraw from confrontation. These communicators allow others to choose and make decisions for them.

personal management skills - The ability to use self-esteem, motivation, goal setting, and personal and career development to excel within an organization.

problem-solving skills - The ability to identify and resolve an inconsistency between an existing and a desired situation.

professionalism - An attitude that is reflected in the way individuals understand and follow business policies and practices, and communicate with others in a workplace environment.

S

stress - The physical or emotional response to a crisis or an unpleasant condition.

T

technical skills - The ability to understand a specific task and to use the tools and techniques related to that task.

time management - The process of planning, recording, and quantifying time spent completing tasks.

time waster - Any activity or behavior that causes more time to be spent on a task than necessary.

V

voice mail - An electronic message system that is accessed by phone.

W

word processing - Using a computer to create, edit, revise, and format written text.

Printed in Great Britain
by Amazon